Comprehension Self-Effi̶c̶i̶e̶n̶c̶y̶, A̶e̶s̶t̶h̶e̶t̶i̶c̶ Reading, and Reader Response

To my brother Ken, his wife Pat and the entire Chiricu clan. This book was possible only through God's Grace!

Love,
Ann

Charlotte Zeitsiff

Comprehension Self-Efficacy, Aesthetic Reading, and Reader Response

Aesthetic Reading, Reader Response, and Students' Literature Comprehension Self-Efficacy Beliefs

LAP LAMBERT Academic Publishing

Impressum / Imprint

Bibliografische Information der Deutschen Nationalbibliothek: Die Deutsche Nationalbibliothek verzeichnet diese Publikation in der Deutschen Nationalbibliografie; detaillierte bibliografische Daten sind im Internet über http://dnb.d-nb.de abrufbar.
Alle in diesem Buch genannten Marken und Produktnamen unterliegen warenzeichen-, marken- oder patentrechtlichem Schutz bzw. sind Warenzeichen oder eingetragene Warenzeichen der jeweiligen Inhaber. Die Wiedergabe von Marken, Produktnamen, Gebrauchsnamen, Handelsnamen, Warenbezeichnungen u.s.w. in diesem Werk berechtigt auch ohne besondere Kennzeichnung nicht zu der Annahme, dass solche Namen im Sinne der Warenzeichen- und Markenschutzgesetzgebung als frei zu betrachten wären und daher von jedermann benutzt werden dürften.

Bibliographic information published by the Deutsche Nationalbibliothek: The Deutsche Nationalbibliothek lists this publication in the Deutsche Nationalbibliografie; detailed bibliographic data are available in the Internet at http://dnb.d-nb.de.
Any brand names and product names mentioned in this book are subject to trademark, brand or patent protection and are trademarks or registered trademarks of their respective holders. The use of brand names, product names, common names, trade names, product descriptions etc. even without a particular marking in this work is in no way to be construed to mean that such names may be regarded as unrestricted in respect of trademark and brand protection legislation and could thus be used by anyone.

Coverbild / Cover image: www.ingimage.com

Verlag / Publisher:
LAP LAMBERT Academic Publishing
ist ein Imprint der / is a trademark of
OmniScriptum GmbH & Co. KG
Heinrich-Böcking-Str. 6-8, 66121 Saarbrücken, Deutschland / Germany
Email: info@lap-publishing.com

Herstellung: siehe letzte Seite /
Printed at: see last page
ISBN: 978-3-659-63626-4

Zugl. / Approved by: Miami, Florida International University, Diss., 2014

TABLE OF CONTENTS

2

3

LIST OF TABLES

DEDICATION

With great love

this work

is

dedicated

to

my husband, Elliot.

Your love and support have been constant,

your belief has been solid,

and

your patience has been endless.

You have sacrificed much to help me achieve this dream.

I will always be grateful, thank you.

ACKNOWLEDGMENTS

During this project I received a great amount of help, and the words on this page are my attempt to express the gratitude that I feel deep within my being. First and foremost, this dissertation is the result of God's Grace and Guidance. With that said, I would like to thank the members of my committee. The kindness, patience, expertise, and professionalism that Dr. Charles Bleiker, Dr. Lynne D. Miller, and Dr. Leonard B. Bliss demonstrated was amazing. In addition to all of these characteristics, Dr. Thomas G. Reio, Jr., my major advisor, was a terrific mentor, who made all the difference in the world. He showed respect for me both as an individual and a professional. When appointments had to be arranged, he was willing to consider my personal and professional schedule in addition to his own; this was remarkable, as was his constant belief in me and my study. I will always be grateful. Thank you, Dr. Reio.

There were many others at FIU whose assistance was of immense value in bringing this dissertation to fruition. Dr. Linda Bliss and Dr. Isadore Newman helped me tremendously during their boot camp sessions. Dr. Linda Bliss's feedback on my drafts was comprehensive and helped me immeasurably. Caprila Almeida and Kaitlyn Pereyra in the OGS office kept me afloat during the whole process. They were marvelous and provided a safe haven from all of the bureaucratic storms. Brandie Thomas in the UGS ETD office patiently and expertly assisted me during the final submission process.

Much gratitude is due to the many colleagues at the site school and to others who provided me with infinite support. Without Tranese Pratt-Lynch and Javier Perez, this study would never have happened, thank you so very much. Collin Bartley always made time for me in his busy schedule and provided meaningful advice and thoughtful, scholarly discussion for which I will always be grateful. Nathasia Mark was always there to lift my spirits. Dr. Malo-Juvera unselfishly assisted me with my proposal. Last, but not least, my love and gratitude to my son, Andrew, and the many other individuals who supported me throughout this whole process. Your prayers and support made the difference; May God Bless You All!

CHAPTER I

INTRODUCTION

Secondary teachers of reading, writing, literature, and language skills, commonly known as English, Language Arts, and Reading (ELAR) teachers, are labeled according to their area or areas of assignment or specialized certification: English (regular and honors), Advanced Placement (AP), Intensive Reading, teachers of English Language Learners (ELL), and Special Education teachers (SPED). Despite these various labels, however, all ELAR teachers face the extraordinary task of following a required and established curriculum as they teach the many aspects of reading, writing, literature, and language. This complex and ever-changing task falls under the overall objective of enabling students to acquire competence in the multiple literacies that exist in today's modern society.

Historically and pedagogically, this field of study is recognized as being extremely critical to academic success in all school subjects. ELAR teachers are held responsible for their students' successful acquisition of numerous skills that have long been accepted as the bases of all academic learning. Moreover, 21st century literacies are more complicated than the literacies of the past. This is because the modes of communication are constantly multiplying and globally expanding due to the rapid advances of technology. These literacies are also more intense in nature, because the speed of delivery is improving as well, such that multiple forms of communication are almost globally instantaneous. A literate person in the 21st century must be competent in a wide and varied range of literacies: using technological tools to communicate globally simultaneously, comprehending and evaluating multi-media texts, as well as maintaining the high level of ethical standards that these very complex literacy environments demand (National Council of Teachers of English [NCTE], 2008). These 21st century literacies also fall under the responsibility of ELAR teachers which further complicates their role.

Background of the Problem

The Testing Era

It has been over a decade since the passing of the controversial No Child Left Behind (NCLB) Act of 2001 (U. S. Department of Education, 2002), President George Bush's reform of federal education policy. This legislation included the mandate that educators must improve student scores on standardized state tests and set the precedent for evaluating our country's education system on the basis of test scores. This political event marked the beginning of the era of high-stakes assessment. President Barack Obama has continued this trend by calling for the distribution of federal funds to be linked to student progress on state assessments, known as the Race to the Top Program (RTTP; U.S. Department of Education, 2009). These two sweeping governmental acts have formed the basis of accountability for all teachers. This era has been defined by a continuing upward spiral of federal and state government intervention in America's education system, which has been increasing in intensity, control, and expense over the years.

Testing and ELAR Teachers

The teaching and learning of the English language arts have been greatly affected by the accountability movement. For ELAR teachers, accountability has now been redefined; primarily, it consists of teachers providing evidence that their students are achieving constant progress as indicated by the students' standardized test scores in reading comprehension and writing. Legislation is forcing teachers to concentrate their efforts on improving the standardized test scores of their students. In some states, like Florida, a teacher's salary will no longer reflect that teacher's particular level of educational accomplishment and number of years of experience. Rather, a teacher's evaluation will be in compliance with the RTTP program which requires that 50% of the evaluation be based on the standardized test performance of the students assigned to that teacher over a three-year period. This landmark change, put into effect in 2011 by Florida Senate Bill, Chapter 2011-1, L.O. F. clearly determined that a teacher's job security will be highly dependent on the success of his/her students; the employment of a teacher will be based on his/her evaluation (Florida Senate Bill, Chapter 2011-1, L. O. F., 2011).

The testing culture that now dominates the educational landscape across our nation has produced a plethora of scripted programs designed to improve student achievement on standardized reading tests (Mathews, 2000). These commercially produced programs require teachers to follow scripts with varying degrees of fidelity (Moustafa & Land, 2002). In most states, as well as in Florida, the setting of this proposed study, teachers are required to use state-adopted textbooks and follow pacing guides for their subject (Miami-Dade County Public Schools [MDCPS], 2012). This creates public school curricula that consist of various types of interactions with textbooks, the accompanying pre-packaged materials, and standardized reading materials. All academic subjects are then to be taught at the designated pace and according to the designated chapters or selections (MDCPS, 2012). The emphasis is placed on students' abilities to master certain skills as indicated by worksheets and/or by answering specific questions, whereas any authentic uses of print are avoided (Edelsky, 1991; Irvine & Larson, 2007).

Authentic Uses of Print

Langer discusses the topic of authentic uses of print in her research study, "Thinking and Doing Literature: An Eight-Year Study" (1998). Perplexed by unanswered questions about the literary mind and hoping to reveal ways that teachers can help students "…think deeply and richly about the works they read." (1998, p. 16), Langer examined the methods readers utilized as they created and embellished their own thoughts during their involvement with a literary piece. This focus led to a search for "...authentic uses of print activities..." (p. 21), activities that encourage and support students' individualized interpretations, thoughts, connections and reactions, before, during, and after their engagement with a text. This research journey revealed five authentic uses of print activities that proved to be successful in literature classrooms: "1) easing access before reading; 2) inviting initial understandings; 3) supporting the development of interpretations; 4) inviting critical stances; and 5) stocktaking" (p. 21).

Langer's previous article, "A Response-Based Approach to Reading Literature" (1994) also included a discussion of "...authentic uses of print activities..." (1998, p. 21). She explained the continuing research "...with teachers struggling to adapt their instruction to a response-based approach to reading literature" (1994, p. 203). The authentic print activities were suggested as optional strategies; each one was developed from the research and created for the purpose of supporting a student-centered, response-based approach to reading literature. In essence, the strategies were designed to help teachers recognize the verbal and nonverbal signals that students expressed as they moved through the process of building their own understandings of the literature. The research indicated that once teachers were able to recognize these signals they were more able to make instructional decisions spontaneously. This, in turn, enabled them to more readily direct students to explore their own meaning-making by: relooking, rethinking, explaining, supporting and/or changing their understandings. As a mode of instruction, this model differed from more traditional instruction because it concentrated on the students' own developing understandings of the literature. One of the important pedagogical developments from this research was the realization that the instructional spontaneity required to effectively guide students in their personal meaning-making journeys carried the prerequisite that class instruction could not be planned or practiced in advance. This instruction could not be based on previous test results or learning experiences; this instruction had to be able to flow as the students developed their understandings (Langer, 1994).

Increasingly, this nontraditional form of instruction, based on students' responses and utilizing authentic uses of print activities, is being pushed aside or ignored to accommodate strategies for skills-mastering that are based on previous test data (MDCPS, 2012; Purves, 1990). This study addressed an area that lies outside the normal perimeters of analyses activated when students fail to make adequate progress on standardized assessments. Whereas many popular analyses focus on particular reading comprehension and vocabulary strategies and how they are used in the instructional setting; this study involved a response-based approach to literature and an authentic use of print activity, reader response. It concentrated on the inclusion of several other factors that have been ignored or dismissed because of the push to raise students' standardized test scores. A briefly detailed discussion of these factors follows: the role that students' self-efficacy beliefs play in their engagement in academic tasks, aesthetic rather than efferent reading of literature, (American literature, for this study), and aesthetically-evoked reader responses to the literature selections.

Testing and Self-Efficacy Beliefs

Students' self-efficacy beliefs is one of the factors commonly ignored when students fail to make adequate progress on standardized reading assessments. This factor was discussed in the studies of Alvermann (2001, 2003) and in the study by Kamil, Intrator, and Kim in 2000, which confirmed that adolescent learners with high self-efficacy, the knowledge that they are capable of succeeding at a task, are more likely to do school-related reading than those who lack this confidence. In addition, Guthrie and Wigfield (2000) indicated that for literacy instruction to be successful, the issues of students' self-efficacy beliefs and engagement must be addressed. The implications of these studies are of particular importance to high school students who must achieve credits in mandatory subjects. In Florida, for example, juniors are mandated to take and pass English 3 to graduate (Florida Department of Education [FLDOE], 2012b).

The English 3 Curriculum and Aesthetic Reading

The problem with the English 3 curriculum in the State of Florida is that it focuses on the chronological study of American literature (FLDOE, 1997; MDCPS, 2012) which presents a considerable challenge for the majority of students for a variety of reasons. It has been the researcher's experience that 11th graders were often lacking the historical background knowledge that they needed to understand the underlying concepts of the literature. The language of the literature is relatively formal for most of the curriculum (MDCPS, 2012), and during the years that the researcher taught the English 3 curriculum it was evident that students had to have a certain level of maturity to be interested in it. Students also repeatedly said that the literature bored them. The literature was rarely easy for even the researcher's best students, and for the many 11th graders in Florida who had not passed the tenth grade

Florida Comprehension Achievement Test (FCAT; FLDOE, 2012a) in reading comprehension, it was very difficult. Moreover, these students were already stigmatized by their failure to read at the 10th grade level, thus the English 3 literature was an additional burden to these students who already had been forced to forfeit an elective in order to take an intensive reading class. Last, but certainly not least, the present curriculum is not diversified in the sense that it fails to offer adequate activities to encourage personal perspectives from students whose origins are reflective of a wide array of racial/ethnic backgrounds (FLDOE, 1997; MDCPS, 2012). Purves (1990) offers an explanation for this void in the curriculum.

> The nation's testing programs devote a great deal of energy to testing reading and writing, but they fail to treat literature and cultural literacy seriously. The artisticaspects of literature and the cultural heritage of our society are not reflected in the nation's tests and as a result lead to neglect by the schools. The tests focus on literal comprehension and on the reading of prose fiction. Poetry and drama are seldom included. (Purves, 1990, p. 1)

It is highly probable that these stipulated problems concerning the English 3 curriculum could have lowering effects on the self-efficacy beliefs of juniors entering the English 3 classroom. Studies by Alvermann (2001, 2003) and Kamil et al. (2000) found that students with high self-efficacy beliefs were more likely to do required reading assignments, and Guthrie and Wigfield (2000) indicated that attention to students' self-efficacy beliefs is one of the indicators of effective literacy instruction. Many English 3 students are already facing the failure of passing the tenth grade reading comprehension test; they often expressed their disenchantment with the lack of activities that engaged their personal perspectives in the researcher's classroom. Such students could have suffered a lowering of their self-efficacy beliefs and hence, may not have been very inclined to do the literature assignments for their English 3 class. This study, therefore, focused on the inclusion of several factors that may have affected high school juniors' levels of self-efficacy relevant to their success in English 3.

Two factors included in this study partially affected the treatment group's levels of self-efficacy regarding the comprehension of American literature and their success in English 3. The first factor was the addition of aesthetic reading of American literature, where the reader's attention focused on what happened between the text and the reader during the literary event (Karolides, 1992; Rosenblatt, 1938, 1978, 1995, 2003). This was in contrast to the conventional efferent, or fact-acquisition reading that the curriculum mandated (MDCPS, 2012). The second factor was an authentic use of print activity, the promotion and acceptance of students' aesthetically-evoked and individualized responses to their reading in the form of written responses. These strategies offered students a means of engaging their personal perspectives as they interacted with the text, instead of engaging the input/output ideology (Edelsky, 1991; Powell, 2009) that has been routinely promoted through the completion of textbook-related worksheets and answering textbook questions. Students were encouraged to read text selections from a personal perspective, select quotes that elicited a particular memory, sensation, or any type of connection, and then write their responses. This study analyzed the effects of this two-part strategy on students' self-efficacy beliefs relevant to their comprehension of American literature and their perceived success in English 3/American literature class. These effects were compared to the same self-efficacy beliefs of students who had been subjected to the conventional input/output ideology of the standard curriculum (MDCPS, 2012).

Following this introduction, the chapter continues with the statement of the problem, the purpose of the study, the significance of the study and the summary of the theoretical background. The delimitations and the research questions conclude the chapter.

Statement of the Problem

Problems with the English 3 Curriculum

The present English 3 curriculum in Florida, American literature, poses a number of challenges to high school juniors. In the researcher's experience, it relies heavily on their, (often inadequate), knowledge of the history of the United States, students are troubled by the language of the literature that seems to be so outdated to them and too formal, many students have demonstrated on the FCAT (FLDOE, 2012a) that they are not capable of reading at the 10th grade level, and students of diverse backgrounds are not provided with a variety of adequate academic, intellectual, and emotional activities to encourage an examination of their personal perspectives.

There are three main factors in this learning marginalization. The first is a random hit or miss selection of mainly excerpt pieces from other cultures. The second is a largely-denied opportunity for the students to read aesthetically, focusing on the reader and text transaction that he/she is individually experiencing during the literary event (Karolides, 1992; Rosenblatt, 1938, 1978, 1995, 2003). The third factor is that students are not usually allowed to respond to the material in a unique aesthetically-evoked reader response that is created from the literary event wherein each "...reader, brings to the transaction a personal linguistic-experiential reservoir, the residue of past transactions in life and language" (Rosenblatt, 1993, p. 381).

Efferent Reading, Aesthetic Reading, Self-Efficacy and Task Mastery

Florida's present English 3 curriculum emphasizes efferently-evoked responses during instruction. Students are expected to look for factual knowledge and then demonstrate that they have gained this knowledge (FLDOE, 2012a, 2012b). This type of reading corresponds to the type of reading that must be mastered to achieve success on standardized tests (Edelsky, 1991; Powell, 2009; Purves, 1990). This type of literacy instruction promotes the process of storing information into the students' minds for the purpose of withdrawing it later. Its purpose is to "…promote ritualized mechanical responses that have little to do with students' lived experiences (Powell, 2009, p. 9). Spears-Bunton and Powell (2009) referred to this type of literacy instruction as "schooled literacy" or simply put, a literacy based on students searching for a singular accurate answer. Students have become very cognizant of the fact that many/most literacy events are designed for the purpose of evaluating them and often do not recognize, or choose not to recognize that literacy experiences could be relevant to their lives. Unable to see relevancy, students often approach their education mechanically, striving to look for the expected correct answers to questions that they perceive to be meaningless (Powell, 2009).

The present English 3 curriculum provides many elements of the "banking education" concept that Freire (1970, 1998) and Freire and Macedo (1987) discussed in their works. They explained that in this type of curriculum, students' minds are regarded as empty and waiting to be filled with knowledge. This concept excludes students' personal connections to the literature that they have acquired through their lived experiences, and this is what occurs when efferent rather than aesthetic reading of the historical literature of America is singularly emphasized (Purves, 1990; Rosenblatt, 1993). This is because it focuses on reading to take away knowledge instead of emphasizing an aesthetic reading event, wherein the "…experience of the reading event is at the center …and what is activated in a reader's mind by the text is much more important than any specific information which remains after the event" (Malo-Juvera, 2012, p. 10).

Efferent reading therefore, is not really a literary event because "…the reader is focused on getting information from the text that can be assimilated for use after reading" (Malo-Juvera, 2012, p. 10). Only the information that the reader has predetermined to be important, like those for answering test questions, is considered by the reader (Malo-Juvera, 2012). This type of reading usually calls to the reader's attention generally-accepted meanings, thus preventing the activation or assimilation of personal ideas or feelings (Rosenblatt, 1995). This study attempted to fill a gap in the literature in that it examined the effects of aesthetic reading and aesthetically-evoked reader responses on students' self-efficacy beliefs about English 3/American literature, research that had not been attempted previously.

13

This study took place in a high school in South Florida that serves as an excellent example of the mixture of racial/ethnic origins and cultures that is reflective of both the community and the county. At the time of the study, the school's student population was approximately 3,300. The population was predominantly Hispanic, (64%), with 14% Non-Hispanic Whites, 21% Non-Hispanic Blacks, and 2% Asian/Indian/Multiracial (FLDOE, 2013b). The promotion of efferent, fact-finding reading and the avoidance of aesthetic, personal reading with this school's population may have had effects on students' success within the English 3/American literature classroom. The studies of Alvermann (2001, 2003) and Kamil et al (2000), indicated that students with a low level of self-efficacy beliefs about reading were more likely to avoid their academic reading assignments. Today, however, because of the emphasis on testing and test preparation, most assignments do not promote or accept students' personal responses. As Guthrie and Wigfield (2000) maintained, literacy instruction must address students' self-efficacy beliefs to be successful, therefore, denying students the opportunity to make personal, aesthetic responses to literature assignments, or to any other academic readings, could potentially have negative effects on their self-efficacy beliefs regarding their comprehension. The historical literature that students normally read efferently for test-taking information was the literature used in this study. The intervention of reading aesthetically and writing aesthetically-evoked reader responses was intended to have effects on students' self-efficacy beliefs. Positively affecting self-efficacy beliefs about comprehension could also have a positive effect on students' success in English 3.

The researcher gave a presentation about the study to each of the six classes that were available for study participation in the convenience sample. The presentations will be described fully in a following chapter. However, one of the discussed topics was grading. It was explained that the classes in the treatment group and the control group would be reading the same literature assignments from the regular pacing guide (MDCPS, 2012), but the treatment group would be taught to read for a different purpose. In addition, the assignments following the reading would not be the same for the two groups. The classes in the control group would do the regular assignments as indicated by the district in the pacing guide and would be graded according to the control group's instructor's grading criteria (2010). The classes in the treatment group, however, would be required to write personal responses to the literature that they read. It was explained that they would be taught how to write the responses, and that there would not be any type of singular, correct answers in this type of response. To receive an A grade on a reader response assignment, the students were told that their responses would have to reveal some sort of personal reaction or connection to the text, and they also had to write the required amount of responses for each assignment. They were also informed that the reader response grades for the treatment group would fulfill the district's grading requirements (2010). The process of allowing and accepting students' written aesthetically-evoked responses, which were recorded as separate reader response assignments in the two column notes format (see Appendix F) after their aesthetic reading, was intended to provide a form of positive feedback to students. This was because the aesthetically-evoked reader responses originated from the reader, were unique, and often received high grades because there were no correct or incorrect responses. Rosenblatt's (1995) sole requirement for the evaluation of aesthetically-evoked reader responses was that the response must somehow link, or connect, with the text.

Students generally interpret high grades as a positive thing, and Bandura (1982, 1986, 1994, 1997) held that positive feedback is a form of instructional confidence-building and could result in increasing students' self-efficacy beliefs about a task. As a positive result of building students' self-efficacy beliefs, students may decide to do their literature assignments (Alvermann, 2001, 2003; Kamil et al., 2000), and one of the requirements for successful literacy instruction would be attained (Guthrie & Wigfield, 2000).

Background Studies

A review of the research revealed some recent studies involving reading self-efficacy beliefs, reading strategies, and reading comprehension. These studies were some examples: McCabe, Kraemer, Miller, Parmar, and Ruscica, 2006; McCrudden, Perkins and Putney, 2005; Naseri, 2012; Nelson and Manset-Williamson, 2006; and Van Keer & Verhaeghe, 2005. Overall, however, there was a dearth of studies regarding the effects on students' self-efficacy beliefs when fictive and non-fictive literature was read aesthetically and aesthetically-evoked reader response strategy was implemented.

Purpose of the Study

The purpose of this study involved the implementation of an instructional strategy that was comprised of two parts. One part of the strategy was the aesthetic reading of American literature, and the second part was the promotion and valuing of students' individualized and unique reader responses to the literature. Its purpose therefore, was to investigate the effects of this two-part instructional strategy on students' overall self-efficacy beliefs relevant to the comprehension of American literature, and consequentially, their success in English 3.

Research Question

The primary research question of this study asked the question, "Is there a relationship between students' participation in aesthetic reading of American literature selections from the required curriculum, students writing aesthetically-evoked responses to these readings as presented in their written responses, and students' self-efficacy beliefs regarding their comprehension of American literature?"

Theoretical Background

Language, Culture, Learning, and the Curriculum

How does one conceptually define language? In 1921, almost a century ago, Edward Sapir stated in his book, *Language: An Introduction to the Study of Speech*, that "Language is the most massive and inclusive art we know" (p. 189). More recently, Lisa Delpit stated, "Our language embraces us long before we are defined by other medium of identity" (2002, p. xix) and then proceeded to remind us that the nuances of a mother's language become part of a developing fetus's identity. Students' vernaculars are rarely accepted as appropriate for written assignments in high school English classes because the curriculum foci are on other areas of written work: standardized grammar use, sentence syntax, adherence to usage rules, and correct concept comprehension and representation. This study promoted and allowed students to concentrate on the expression of their personal reactions and impressions to the literature, instead of focusing on their grammar, spelling, usage, or whether or not they identified the information they need for answering test questions. This acceptance of their thoughts, emotions, and language regarding the literature was for the purpose of offering students the possibility of gaining the self-efficacy benefits of succeeding in the literature task (Bandura, 1982, 1986, 1994, 1997).

The history of literature in the secondary curriculum forms the second part of the theoretical foundation of this proposed study. It explains how the curriculum became what it is today. By juxtaposing this history with Freire's (1970) concept of democratic schooling, it will become clear to the reader that public education in America is really not very democratic and has some similarities to Freire's "banking concept of education" (1970, p. 58). In addition, the place of literature in today's curriculum reflects a variety of social perceptions that are related to power. Some regard these perceptions as the promotion of certain designated groups over others. These conceptualizations involve a wide array of past and present democratic ideologies, webbed within and around a confusing mass of perceptions that often include, but are not limited to, race, culture, and gender (Spears-Bunton, 1992).

Reader Response

The aesthetic stance towards literature, and aesthetically-evoked responses to literature was formally introduced to the world of English language educators by Louise Rosenblatt in her first edition of *Literature as Exploration* in 1938. The theory she proposed argued that the reader and the text, in that particular setting and time, results in a transaction that occurs along a continuum that ranges from efferent to aesthetic. The promotion of aesthetically-evoked responses to literature, therefore, allows a student to react to what is happening between him/her and the text during the literary event that is taking place at that unique moment in time. These reader responses are individualized and are evidence of the transaction that is occurring in that specific timeframe. The only real provision that Rosenblatt offered is that the literature must support the response in some way. In other words, the student should be able to justify his/her response as it pertains to the particular text or part of the text (Rosenblatt, 1995). Because these strategies are not efferent, (test-taking) strategies, but aesthetic, (transactions between the reader, the connections the reader is making, and the text), (Rosenblatt, 1995), they are of low priority and usually avoided in today's high-stakes classrooms. This perspective, that instructional efforts in literature are almost always focused on directing students towards the attainment of predetermined understandings of literature was also expressed in Applebee's (1993) research on literature classrooms throughout the nation.

As an authentic use of print activity, aesthetically-evoked reader responses are written representations of transactions between the reader, the connections the reader is making, and the text (Rosenblatt, 1995). These responses, if completed, also provide a means of task mastery which has proven to be significant in the building of self-efficacy beliefs of students (Bandura, 1982, 1986, 1997). This study supported Bandura's task mastery research (1982, 1986, 1997) by specifying the grading criteria to students that would result in a grade of A. These criteria were the completion of the assignment by writing the specific number of required responses upon the completion of an aesthetic reading assignment and showing your personal connections, reactions, etc. to the text in your responses.

In this study, it was expected that the acceptance of perspectives from students from a variety of cultures and experiences in the form of aesthetically-evoked reader responses would enable these students to gain confidence in their ability to succeed at the task of comprehending the literature.

Self-Efficacy and Task Mastery

The concept of self-efficacy was an integral part of this study. Bandura defined self-efficacy as "people's judgments of their capabilities to organize and execute courses of action required to attain designated types of performances" (Bandura,

1986, p. 391). Self-efficacy is central in the psychological functioning of human agency, the feeling that a person can influence his/her life and the lives of others (Bandura, 1982; Bandura & Schunk, 1981; Schunk, 2004). Studies (Bandura, 1997; Schunk & Pajares, 1995) have shown that the influence of self-efficacy beliefs extends to multiple areas of a person's life: task choice, effort, motivation, persistence, resilience, and achievement. Bandura (1994) also argued that of the many parts involved in individuals' systems of self-knowledge, the part that has the greatest influence on people's lives is the individual's concept of self-efficacy.

Particularly relevant to this study were Bandura's (1982, 1994) assertions that mastery experience is an extremely powerful source of positive self-efficacy beliefs, and the mastery of a task is also the best source of positive self-efficacy beliefs. Students' completed reader response assignments were intended to serve as mastery task experiences in this study. The completed response assignments of study participants in the English 3 regular classes that made-up the intervention group were encouraged and accepted following the aesthetic reading of American literature pieces. It was expected that each student's interpretations of the texts would vary because each reader would have his/her own set of experiences, (past and present), global views, prejudices, purposes for reading, and present state of mind. This study proposed that students would experience the mastery of comprehending the literature from their own unique perspectives. This would be accomplished by completing the assigned number of aesthetically-evoked reader responses, and in turn, result in higher self-efficacy beliefs regarding their comprehension of American literature and promote their success with English 3/American literature.

Significance of the Study

A major component of the existing democratic society in the United States is the role of education, and educators are responsible for developing strategies that support the constitutional rights of a free and equal education for all. Public schools however, have embraced schooled literacy and the curriculum significantly reflects the banking model that Freire (1970) described. The existing foci of the English 3 curriculum are efferent reading and responding to canonical American literature because these foci require answers that correlate with predetermined correct answers, like those required by standardized test questions (Applebee, 1993). Students cannot draw upon their personal reactions to texts, and this can alienate some students. Hence, this emphasis is a form of test preparation and could be interpreted as an example of hegemony in the curriculum, "...a process in which dominant groups in society come together to form a bloc and sustain leadership over subordinate groups" (Apple, 1996, p. 14). This study was designed to draw attention to the hegemonic facets of the existing secondary English curriculum and more specifically, the

18

English 3 curriculum. It was also undertaken to shed some light on the destructive forces of hegemony and attempted to show the positive effects of promoting individualized interactions with literature. Authentic use of print activities, like the reader responses in this study, attached positive values to all students' voices. This added to the educational discussion of enabling all students to be heard, and also supported the constitutional rights of all people in our nation to receive an equal and democratic education.

This study was significant in that it provided data on high school juniors. These data provided information about the self-efficacy beliefs of these students regarding their comprehension of American literature and English 3, and the relationship of these beliefs to particular facets of the English 3 curriculum. Data from this study added to many relevant discussions: teaching strategies that have effects on student success, strategies that invite all students to become engaged in literature, the relationship of self-efficacy beliefs and the creation of positive momentum towards graduation, and finally, the recognition that the curriculum's emphasis on efferent reading and responding may have severely destructive consequences for students. This is based on the knowledge that questions that are formulated like standardized test questions emphasize reading comprehension from the input/output perspective; test-takers are rarely required to analyze, interpret, evaluate, or connect personally to the text (Purves, 1990).

This study had a number of practical implications which added to its scientific merit. Cullinan (2000) showed that students may not develop a love of reading from the way reading is experienced in school, and Irving (1980) indicated that the connection between reading and pleasure does not exist for many students. The current high school curriculum presents reading to students with a variety of punitive measures attached (e.g., grades, high-stakes tests, test-retaking, failure to graduate because of failure on standardized tests). It is understandable, therefore, that so many students conclude that reading is not enjoyable and/or they are poor at the task of reading. As Bandura (1982, 1994) indicated, one's perceived failure to master a task has great effects on one's self-efficacy beliefs. This study offered an alternative way of presenting reading to students that promoted an individualized, authentic use of print, ergo, genuine, (and hopefully), positive literacy experience. This study examined the effects on students' self-efficacy beliefs regarding American literature as they participated in the aesthetic reading and the aesthetically-evoked writing of reader responses. The written reading responses were the vehicles through which students expressed and explained their transactions with the text. This study invited teachers to become instruments of social change for the purpose of improving the educational experience for all students.

Delimitations of the Study

To delimit a research study is to clarify the scope of the proposed study (Creswell, 2005). Although for the purpose of generalizing it would best to examine all 11th grade students enrolled in regular English 3/American literature class, this study is delimited to 11th grade students who were enrolled in regular English 3/American literature class at a single, Title 1, magnet high school located in a section of South Florida that is predominantly Hispanic.

Study Terms and Phrases

Academic Success is achieving above the bare minimum to receive credit, the attainment of a grade of C or better for the year.

Aesthetic Reading is reading as an individualized and unique transaction with the text that is particular to that place in time and with that particular individual.

Authentic Use of Print Activities are activities that are designed to encourage and support each student's individualized interpretations, thoughts, reactions, connections, (etc.) before, during, and after their engagement with a text.

Efferent Reading is reading to gather information, deemed to be necessary for standardized test-taking by the proponents of the high stakes educational curriculum.

Literacy refers to the many aspects of reading, writing, literature, and language. This also includes the ability to: globally communicate using technology, communicate across cultures, simultaneously assimilate and analyze multiple streams of information, and comprehend and evaluate multi-media texts. This literacy also means the maintenance of the high level of ethical standards that these very complex literacy environments demand (National Council of Teachers of English, 2008).

Mastery Experiences are a source of self-efficacy information that is based on one's successful performance of a task (Bandura, 1986, p. 399).

Reading Comprehension is the ability to connect discrete bits of information from a text in order to construct meaning (Goodman, 1982).

Self-Efficacy is a person's judgment of his/her own capabilities to perform tasks at a certain level (Bandura, 1994).

CHAPTER II

LITERATURE REVIEW

This review of literature establishes the theoretical foundations of the study, and it begins with a historical look at the events that led to the era of high stakes testing and accountability that is presently driving the public education system in America today. The review then explores the history of the English curriculum in the United States and the foundations of the English 3 curriculum. This is followed by a review of some of the important consequences for high school students arising from the interplay of the high-stakes testing and the English curriculum. Next, there is a review of the theory of reader response and the phenomenon of aesthetic transactions with text. Finally, the research regarding individuals' self-efficacy beliefs is explored.

High-Stakes Testing and Accountability

The United States is now two hundred and thirty-eight years old, and its education system is currently experiencing the highest level of government intervention and control in history with the implementation of the NCLB of 2001 (U. S. Department of Education, 2002), the RTTP (U. S. Department of Education, 2009), and most recently, the implementation of the Common Core State Standards (CCSS; NGACBP & CCSSO, 2010). In 1957, over five decades in the past, the legislation that actually began this trend was put into effect. The Russians had successfully launched the very first satellite, Sputnik, and the Race for Space had begun! The United States government mandated spending in all the basic subject areas such as literacy and mathematics, but the greatest focus was on science education (Bernard & Mondale, 2001).

Twenty-four years later, in 1981, President Reagan responded to evidence that the educational system in the United States was showing signs of inferiority to some other industrialized nations' educational systems by requesting a full-scale educational assessment (Bernard & Mondale, 2001). This extremely large task was assigned to the National Commission of Excellence in Education (NCEE) by the United States Department of Education. The commission was directed to make adolescents a priority; therefore, high schools received particular attention. There were three other areas of education that were particularly reviewed: early elementary schooling, postsecondary education, and the specialized programs of vocational and technical education (NCEE, 1983).

Although the results of the national assessment have since been disputed by at least one faction (Rothstein, 2008), the resulting document, *A Nation at Risk* (NCEE, 1983) included reviews of these areas of each level of education: educational expectations, the curriculum content that was being offered to students, the quality of teaching that was in place, and the amount of time required of students to ensure success in school. The findings revealed that our nation's system was lacking in all four areas to the extent that the President suggested that if a foreign nation had tried to impose the existing system on the people of the United States, the citizenry would consider it an act of war (NCEE, 1983).

The findings of the commission revealed a considerable amount of disturbing information. U. S. students did not place first or second on any of the 19 academic tests that were used to compare them with international students. Twenty-three million adults and 13% of 17-year-olds were functionally illiterate with as many as 40% of the nation's minority youth in this category. Other statistics showed that SAT test scores had deteriorated considerably on both the verbal and mathematics portions since 1963, as well as the fact that many 17-year-olds were deficient in higher-order thinking skills. In addition, business and military leaders reported that millions of dollars must be spent on remedial/training programs in the basic skills of literacy and mathematics to prepare their new personnel for entry into training programs. Overall, the report offered proof that the educational system was deficient in substance, rigor, and proof of mastery requirements (NCEE, 1983).

President Reagan reacted to the findings in the document, *A Nation at Risk* (NCEE, 1983), by implementing a program of national educational reform involving increased accountability in the basic skills areas of reading, writing, mathematics and science. Priorities were placed on grading that demonstrated levels of student mastery, rigorous secondary and postsecondary examinations and graduation requirements, and college entrance requirements that supported the higher levels of high school subject mastery. Reagan was the first American president to order a comprehensive evaluation of the educational system, and the findings of the evaluation provided the catalyst for the first national program of educational reform.

In 2001, President George Bush reinforced the emphasis on educational accountability in the controversial NCLB of 2001 (U. S. Department of Education, 2002) reform policy, utilizing the scores in the evaluation areas of reading comprehension, writing, and mathematics as the bases of this legislation. The purpose of this federal policy was clearly stated, "To close the achievement gap with accountability, flexibility, and choice, so that no child is left behind (2002, title page). This legislation also included the mandate that educators must improve students' scores on the standardized state tests in those designated areas of reading, writing, and mathematics. There was also a provision requiring each state to create a timeline outlining its plan for achieving the goal of 100% student proficiency on state assessment tests by the end of the 2013-2014 school year. This legislation allowed each state to determine proficiency levels for its students as well as the level of difficulty of its tests. Nevertheless, annual goals for proficiency were to be determined in each timeline. The end of the 2007-2008 school year marked the half-way point in the time interval for students to achieve proficiency, and the achievement timeline for almost half of the states, (23), indicated that the steepest gains in the achievement levels had been scheduled for the second half of the time period (Kroger, Campbell, Thacker, Becker & Wise, 2007). In other words, for many states, a tremendous amount of work was going to be necessary between 2008 and 2014 if states were going to meet their timelines. Achievement of the highest gains would have to be necessary during that time interval (Kroger et al., 2007).

President Bush's NCLB (U. S. Department of Education, 2002) legislation set the precedent for evaluating the entire education system of the United States on the basis of standardized test scores; the accountability era has continued throughout President Barack Obama's administration which has been defined by more standardized testing through the implementation of several legislative pieces. The RTTP (U. S. Department of Education, 2009), links the distribution of federal funds to student progress on state assessments, which continues to have a wide range of effects on all aspects of public education: students, parents, schools, school systems and every state's legislation. The other legislative piece promoted the drive to nationalize education through the establishment of Common Core State Standards (CCSSI), and was authored as a combined effort of two groups located in Washington, D. C., the National Governors Association Center for Best Practices (NGACBP) and the Council of Chief State School Officers (CCSSO; NGACBP & CCSSO, 2010).

> The standards clearly communicate what is expected of students at each grade level. This will allow our teachers to be better equipped to know exactly what they need to help students learn and establish individualized benchmarks for them. The Common Core State Standards focus on core conceptual understandings and procedures starting in the early grades, thus enabling teachers to take the time needed to teach core concepts and procedures well-and to give students the opportunity to master them. (NGACBP & CCSSO, 2010, p. 1)

Although this legislation was state-based, with each state determining whether it wanted to participate or not, it was federally-linked because federal monies were connected to state participation (2010).

ELAR Teachers and Accountability

These governmental acts have formed the basis of accountability for all teachers, and for ELAR teachers, accountability has been defined as evidence of constantly improving student achievement indicated by continuously improving standardized test scores in reading comprehension and writing. Hence, this method of accountability has become the driving force behind educational reform and the continuing era of high-stakes testing in American education.

The era of high-stakes testing has brought about other changes in the teaching profession. Most recently, in Florida, like many other states, the next few years will reveal significant changes in the way teachers are paid. Contracted salaries are being replaced by the distribution of money according to the mandates of the RTTP (U. S. Department of Education, 2009) legislation, which requires that 50% of each teacher's evaluation be determined by his/her students' progress on standardized tests. This is a critical change because in Florida, as in many other states, a teacher's employment will be based on the same evaluation (Florida Senate Bill, Chapter 2011-1, L.O. F., 2011).

It is evident that the era of high-stakes testing and accountability has reached a new level, but it is also evident to many in the field of education that accountability which is based on standardized test scores has a plethora of problems (Hayes, 2013). The focus of public education has become student performance on standardized tests, which, in Florida, are called The Florida Comprehensive Achievement Tests in Reading, Math, and Writing (FCAT; FLDOE, 2012a). Like most states, this focus has produced multi-leveled and complex changes for education and educators: teachers are required to attend more professional development sessions, classroom visits from the state and district are more frequent and demanding, adherence to instructional guides for content and pacing is monitored, and scripted programs are prescribed with the expectation that teachers will adhere to the program. The criteria for lesson plans, grading rubrics, and the filing of students' work are determined by the district and/or the state, and to receive a satisfactory evaluation, teacher compliance is necessary (Florida Senate Bill, Chapter 2011-1, L.O. F., 2011).

The era of high-stakes testing and accountability has significantly influenced the curricula of language arts classrooms. The NCLB (U. S. Department of Education, 2002) legislation mandated testing in both reading and mathematics for students in grades 3-8, and for grade10 in high school. Each state has its own guidelines for students who fail these tests. In Florida, students who do not pass the FCAT in grade 3 are retained, and the consequence for graduating seniors who do not pass the FCAT is severe. Every year, over 4% of the students who are designated as standard diploma students receive a Certificate of Completion instead (Florida Department of Education, 2012c). Both of these consequences serve as examples of the ramifications of students failing to master a task, and task mastery is essential to building self-efficacy beliefs (Bandura, 1982, 1986, 1994, 1997), which in turn has been linked to reading performance and achievement (Alvermann, 2001, 2003; Kamil et al, 2000), as well as an indicator of successful literacy instruction (Guthrie & Wigfield, 2000). Poorer self-efficacy beliefs in reading and other academic domains, such as math and writing, are powerfully linked to poorer performance on academic tasks in general (Alvermann, 2001, 2003; Bandura, 1997; Pajares, 1997). A logical conclusion would be the probability that students who fail the FCAT, especially those who fail repeatedly, experience lowered self-efficacy beliefs about possessing the skills required to pass.

In addition, many states have agreed to the Common Core Standards Initiative "…led by the National Governors Association Center for Best Practices (NGA Center) and the Council of Chief State School Officers" (CCSSC; NGACBP & CCSSO, 2010, p. 1). The purpose of this initiative was to gather the highest quality standards information from across the country, and to use this information to develop educational standards for K-12 that will be used uniformly across the nation. Although the Common Core Standards Initiative (2010) denies that this movement will result in nationalized education, many educators predict that it will at least lead to a nation-wide reading test for the purpose of providing data for state-to-state comparison (Hayes, 2013). Add the RTTP (U. S. Department of Education, 2009) to the picture, which implemented the addition of student performance on tests as one of the bases for teachers' pay, and the end result is language arts curricula that are drill and test curricula, developed for the purpose of teaching students how to answer questions after reading short passages (Brophy, 1990).

Teachers' fears regarding these test-based curricula, led the President of the National Council of Teachers of English (NCTE), Sandy Hayes (2013) to state, "…we join organizations like AFT…in calling for a moratorium on standardized testing and immediate suspension for the practice of evaluating teachers based on student scores on standardized tests" (p.1). A particularly problematic element of this test-based curriculum for ELAR teachers is that the questions on these high-stakes tests do not require students to make personal connections, analyze, or interpret (Purves, 1990). This test-based reading experience is efferent reading, and its primary purpose is to deposit information into students' minds for later assessment, as opposed to aesthetic reading which focuses on the acceptance of learners' feelings, experiences, judgments, and logical connections. The emphasis is on a singular response, and students do not see or feel any connection to their lives when they participate in these types of literary experiences (Powell, 2009). When students focus their efforts on trying to provide an answer that a teacher, professor, or some other authority has pre-designated as the right answer, the concepts of reading for enjoyment, interest, or personal connections lose importance (Rosenblatt, 1995). This concentration on efferent reading is a direct result of the high-stakes testing and accountability era in our education system (Mathews, 2000), and may be a likely influence on lowering students' self-efficacy beliefs about reading and their subsequent performance on reading tasks (Bandura, 1982, 1986, 1994, 1997).

English, Literature, and the Secondary English Curriculum

The place of literature in the secondary school curriculum is complicated because of the involvement of multiple facets. It involves the general history of English as a school subject, the changing roles of both English and the literature teacher, and the development of public education within the parameters of an emerging nation based on the principles of equality and democracy. English Language Arts/Reading has been at the forefront of education more than any other academic subject in American education and continues to take-up at least 50% of classroom time (Applebee, 1974; Marshall, 1987). This fact stands today as well; the reading/language arts were given priority status by both the NCLB (U. S. Department of Education, 2002) legislation and the RTTP (U. S. Department of Education, 2009). As a result of this attention, this field continues to undergo constant scrutiny and criticism.

Knowledge of the history of English and the history of the English curriculum in the United States is useful in understanding the bases of this study; it sheds light on some of the problems that plague this most critical subject area. Beginning around the year 1750, and continuing for about 115 years to the end of the Civil War, 1865, English in high school was closely modeled after the British college curriculum. The emphasis was on schooling young, White men to be literate and scholarly, evidenced by the ability to memorize long rhetorical passages and present these passages in the correct oratorical style. Examinations were conducted in the same format, and starting in the early 1800s, literature was viewed as privileged information and something that was dangerous for young minds because it was presumed that immoral subjects or concepts that were otherwise not acceptable may be discussed within the text. As a consequence of that mind-frame, literature was taught with great restrictions. Instructors chose selections based on the religious value that the text offered. The intention was to cement morals and values into the heads of students (Applebee, 1974; Spring, 1997).

Although this British-based approach to English continued into the 1800s, the end of the 1700s had coincided with the advent of the Romantic period which was characterized by several emphases: "...strong emotion, the imagination, freedom from classical correctness in art forms, and rebellion against social conventions" (Houghton Mifflin, 1988, p. 1018). By the late 1800s this era was in full swing, and it was during this time that literature finally qualified as a major school subject; it was recognized as a source of cultural values and social mores. The duality of this concept became evident with the realization that if literature could promote positive ethics and standards, then it could also promote negative morality. The powerful role of literature in the classroom had come to light and educators recognized that literature could promote social/cultural beliefs and ideologies. These beliefs suffused the general and educational discourse of the colonial times, and it defined the colonial *White* person; everyone else was defined as the colonial other person.

> …the idea of the colonized 'other' being wholly and hierarchically different from the 'white self'. In inventing discursively the colonial 'other,' whites were parasitically producing an apparently stable western white self out of a previously non-existent self. Thus, the western (read white) self and the colonial 'other' were both products of discursive construction. (Fine, Weis, & Addelson, 1998, p. 151)

This discursively-created identity was specifically for White males and was accepted as the cultural identity for the new nation known as America. It was this identity that was targeted for education, to the exclusion of almost all others (Morrison, 1992).

Based on this cultural identity that was formed in the colonial times, White males became the privileged group in society. They were the ones who were educated and prepared to assume the positions of leadership in the country. According to Frankenberg (1993), this cultural identity and its assumed sense of privilege defined Whiteness and became the acceptable standard for the American way of life. For the most part, this was not recognized as a problem by White/Western people and continues to be strongly represented today. Frankenberg also found that a by-product of this accepted standard was the notion that all others should be excluded from the educational scene. This was exemplified by the fact that post slavery, literacy, (learning or teaching), for African Americans was criminalized, and the vestiges of those laws continued into the 1900s (Frankenberg, 1993).

The majority of academics believed that "imaginative literature posed a real threat to the moral well-being of its readers" (Applebee, 1974, p. 21) previous to the development of the literary canon in the very late 1800s. This belief held that a power existed within literature enabling it to change individuals' behaviors and ideologies such that literature of any kind was suspect. This same train of thought influenced the founders of the literary canon, known as the Committee of Ten. This group of educational scholars was appointed by the National Education Association in 1892, and they were given the task of studying the entire field of secondary education. The President of Harvard University, Dr. Charles W. Elliot, accepted the chairmanship of this committee and directed the appointment of nine other subcommittees for the purpose of studying the nine major subject areas (National Education Association, 1893).

The importance of the Committee of Ten's final report was that it established a general framework for discussion of the goals of secondary education. In many ways, the report of the committee reflected the crossroad between an educational system designed to provide everyone with a common education and an educational system organized to provide everyone with a specific education based on a future social destination. (Spring, 1997, p. 223)

Many educators believe that the committee's final report transformed literature into a definite political entity, and a means of social control and cultural transmission; this definition of literacy still fits in many places in the world today (Freire & Macedo, 1987). This point has been debated by the fact that the Committee of Ten also had addressed the question of whether students in high school who were not planning to go to college should receive the same education as students who were planning to attend college. The fact that the committee's report indicated that all students in secondary school should receive the same education created an intense debate because the social implications of this decision were very clear; the committee had decided that all students, (poor or wealthy), deserved to receive the same education (Spring, 1997).

The secondary English Curriculum, the literary canon, however, reflected the social patterns of the times, and education was directed to all White males. It is also true that during the course of our nation's history this canon has been maintained by those who have the most power. Traditionally, the powerful have not been people of color or women. One can recognize, therefore, that the place of literature in the secondary curriculum is a reflection of political, economical, and social conceptualizations of power and control that can be perceived as the promotion of the domination of certain groups over others (Delpit, 1988; Spears-Bunton, 1992; Spears-Bunton & Powell, 2009). The English curriculum today has some remnants of this reflection of various forms of power, and this is particularly obvious by the push to concentrate on test-taking literacy skills, efferent reading and answering. The pressure for students to excel on standardized reading tests has over-shadowed the idea of helping students learn to read for pleasure. This is an example of a "schooled literacy" (Spears-Bunton & Powell, 2009, p. 6). It is a literacy that is strong in the promotion of the ideas of those who have been, and are now in power. These powers have created a literacy curriculum that serves as a means to achieve the end that they desire. It is not a literacy that is based on other realities, like the reality of the existence of the many and varied social and cultural groups (Freire & Macedo, 1987) or the reality that a student who can read for enjoyment can build self-efficacy beliefs about reading by simply becoming engaged and succeeding in the reading task

(Alvermann, 2001, 2003; Bandura, 1982, 1986, 1994, 1997; Kamil et al., 2000; Linnenbrink & Pintrich, 2003; Pintrich & Schunk, 2002).

There is evidence that this type of literacy has been promoted for many years as was revealed in Anyon's (1980) description of a public school language arts curriculum. The described schools were in an environment of moderate, (working-class), socio-economic status. Her study revealed that the classroom environments subjected students to dictated reading choices and publisher-made worksheets. Thirty-four years later it seems that educators are still dealing with the same narrow-minded mindset.

The present form of literacy that appears in today's test-taking curriculum, falls in line with Freire's "banking concept of education" (Freire, 1970, p. 58) wherein students' minds are perceived as empty vessels waiting to be filled, rather than minds that are rich with all sorts of personal experiences, cultural schemas, artifacts, and history. This ideology can promote a disconnect from schooling for many of today's students who find little relevance in the curriculum to their lived experiences. Minority students may be especially vulnerable to this type of curriculum because the relevance to their lives may be even more distant than it is to other students (Spears-Bunton & Powell, 2009).

The connections between Freire's "banking concept of education" (1970, p. 58), Spears-Bunton & Powell's "schooled literacy" (2009, p. 6) theory, and the reality of the high-stakes testing era in our nation's education provide insight into the secondary English curriculum. An analysis of the present curriculum reveals that to attain literacy, students are usually subjected to either a curriculum that devotes a disproportionate amount of time on reading skill drills or a curriculum that simply serves as a means of preserving things as they are. The first curriculum avoids creative, critical insight that fosters discussion and personal revelations; the second simply presents the values of the dominant group as what is best for the country, and therefore all of us (Cadiero-Kaplan, 2002).

Reading classes are part of the secondary English curriculum and the format is comprised of reading skills work and commercial reading skills programs. The format for the English classes is a combination of the reading skills objectives and using literature to promote test-taking skills. The promotion of efferent reading of texts ignores students' personal connections to the texts and often alienates them because it makes them feel like their own impressions and opinions do not count (Rosenblatt, 1938, 1995). Seeman's (1959) research held that an individual that feels alienated experiences a decrease in his/her self-efficacy beliefs (Seeman, 1959). Students can feel alienated in a reading class because the focus is on test-taking-type questions and answers, efferent reading and answering, and what they feel or experience through the text is ignored (MDCPS, 2012). Aesthetic reading and

29

responding promotes the acceptance of students' feelings, connections, impressions and opinions about the text; students cannot give wrong answers as long as there is some sort of logical connection to the text (Rosenblatt, 1938, 1995). Aesthetic reading and answering therefore promotes self-efficacy beliefs about reading because if students do the assignments, they are able to achieve academically and therefore master the task (Alvermann, 2001, 2003; Bandura, 1986, 1994, 1997; Kamil et al., 2000; Pintrich & Schunk, 2002). In contrast, efferent reading promotes a test-taking mentality, and perhaps all students are not confident with that frame of mind.

In Paulo Freire's works, *Pedagogy of the Oppressed*, (1970) and *Teachers as Cultural Workers*, (1998) as well as in his work with Donaldo Macedo, *Literacy, Reading the Word & the World*, (1987), the concept of education as a pathway to freedom was a main theme. Freire explained that when oppressors deposit what they consider to be knowledge into those that they oppress, they are simply projecting their own ignorance onto others. This ideology simply produces passivity and suppresses the conscious minds of the oppressed. This loss of cultural, communal, and individual identity in turn promotes an atmosphere of alienation and a receptiveness to welfare, which in turn keeps the oppressed from recognizing themselves as being worthy of attaining liberation, a true state of humanness. Freire insisted that a system of education that thrives on the control by a dominant group simply indoctrinates the oppressed into adapting to the world of oppression; it kills the individual's creativity, the essence of life (Freire, 1970, 1998; Freire & Macedo, 1987). It may be that teachers are forced into this indoctrination because they are required to follow the designated curriculum that emphasizes efferent reading and responding rather than aesthetic reading and responding. This can successfully alienate students by ignoring their creative and personal impressions and reactions to what they read (Rosenblatt, 1995).

Freire's concept of education promoted a joint dialogue between teachers and students, wherein there is a mutual responsibility for the creation of true knowledge. This knowledge is to be created through the pursuit of full humanity for all humans, a system of "problem-posing education" (1970, p. 73), based on the genuine respect and inclusion of the world views of all people; the content of this education would be the people's perceptions of reality. Once these realities are determined, the focus would be on the accumulation of practical knowledge for the purpose of understanding the world. Freire considered this educational concept as the definition of democratic schooling (1998).

By definition, the "problem-posing education" (Freire, 1970, p. 73) that Freire promoted had as its founding principle, the act of respecting the world views and perceptions of others. "Yet one of the principal [sic] unresolved issues in Freire's work was its dialectical technique of binary opposition (e.g., oppressor/oppressed, monologue and dialogue), and the absence of an elaborated model of text and language" (Luke, 2012, p.6). This concept of education would, however, require that, "The alternative is to begin from learners' worldviews, in effect turning them into inventors of the curriculum, critics and creators of knowledge" (p. 7). This proposed ideology is contrary to the existing curriculum in our schools today because the emphasis on test-taking instruction, efferent reading and responding, supersedes anything else that the curriculum may offer. How students view their world or the world in general is of low priority in all curricula (U. S. Department of Education, 2012). Unfortunately for Florida's students who are in the 11th grade, this fact is particularly evident and obvious in the English 3 curriculum (MDCPS, 2012).

English 3

Across the nation, students in their third year of high school usually take an English class that is similar to English 3 in the State of Florida. In this state it is one of the four annual English courses that must be taken and passed for a student to graduate (Florida Department of Education, 2012b). Twenty-first century high school students have a superfluity of challenges; however, juniors are faced with a considerable number of academic challenges that fall within the English, and thus the state, curriculum. Those who failed to master the state reading comprehension test in the 10th grade are required to forfeit an elective to take an Intensive Reading class (Florida Department of Education, 2012b; U. S. Department of Education, 2002). They are stigmatized by this; all of their subject area teachers are made aware of their failure. Their peers know of their failure as well because of their placement in these classes. As an added burden, these students are often forced to take special ACT/SAT preparation classes which they often regard as *another reading class*. Last, but certainly not least, all juniors must pass English 3, which focuses on the chronological study of American literature, a considerable challenge for most students (Florida Department of Education, 1997; MDCPS, 2012).

The English 3 curriculum in Florida presents significant challenges to even the best students, and is extremely difficult for many students, evidenced by the fact that over 12,000 students in the state of Florida failed to qualify for promotion to 12th grade in 2010 (Florida Department of Education, 2011a). Perhaps the curriculum, a historical study of American literature fails to interest them, or maybe their often-expressed dislike of the older, more formal language of some of the literature presents the biggest problem, but whatever the reason, in Florida, close to 30% of high school juniors fail English 3 the first time they take it (Florida Department of Education, 2012c).

The regular English 3 classes are mainly comprised of students who have not passed the 10th grade state reading assessment, the FCAT (Florida Department of Education, 2012a); these students have particular problems with simply reading the required literature because they cannot read at the 10th grade level. These students are already stigmatized by their failure on the assessment test because they are placed in special reading classes, and their difficulties with comprehending the literature certainly does not boost the morale of these students. Such task failures are likely to lower these students' self-efficacy beliefs regarding their success in English 3 (Bandura, 1982, 1997; Schunk & Pajares, 1995).

The English 3 curriculum is similar to the English curriculum in general in the sense that it focuses on efferently-evoked responses during classroom instruction and activities that are efferent-based; the curriculum is designed to support reading for test-taking. This fact does not help students who are already having self-efficacy issues regarding reading comprehension. The curriculum activities require that teachers repeatedly ask students to find that one correct answer (MDCPS, 2012), and many students have difficulty doing so. This cycle of being unable to succeed adequately in comprehension activities and therefore maybe suffering another task failure may correspond to a lowering of students' self-efficacy beliefs (Bandura, 1982, 1997; Schunk & Pajares, 1995). Furthermore, this focus on retaining factual information from the literature that students read promotes a comprehension that is mechanical, superficial, and very often meaningless to their lives (Rosenblatt, 1938, 1995). With the emphasis on reading for test-taking, students do not enter into an emotional or empathetic transaction with the text because they are denied an engagement with the text that is personal (1938, 1995). Academic difficulties in English 3 class may result in the failure to receive credit for English 3 during the school year; this would prevent a student from being classified as a senior when they return the next school year. The English 3 credit must be accomplished in one way or another: credit recovery class, adult night school, virtual school, or repeating the class during their senior year. A student who fails to make-up the English 3 credit does not graduate (Florida Department of Education, 2012b).

Reader Response

Several types of reader response are discussed in the literary community; however, the type that was used in this study reflected the "Reader-Plus-Text-Oriented" (Rosenblatt, 2003, p. 70) theory of Louise Rosenblatt's. This theory was first explained in her book, Literature as Exploration, published in 1938. What is particularly significant about the publication date of this first theoretical book on reader response theory is the fact that her work did not represent the accepted literary theory of the time. For the most part, the academic community ignored Rosenblatt's theory until well after World War II ended in 1945 (Allen, 1991).

The road to acceptance of Rosenblatt's theory in the literacy community, as it was described in Literature as Exploration (1938), was long and complicated. This acceptance was also incomplete; as is often the norm in education, there always seems to be those who find it too difficult to break away from the traditional methods of instruction. Although this reticence to change is often the normal course of events in academia, the field of literacy education in the United States, has proven to be susceptible to this type of diehard attitude over the years of this country's existence (Chall, 1967).

Historically, the tenants of the Committee of Ten's final report (National Education Association, 1893), and the resulting literary canon set the course and pace of the secondary English curriculum until the end of World War I. During this time period, one of the traditional approaches to literature was established. Its foundations were "Teaching literature, from the biographical-historical vantage point, has [sic] focused on the life and times of the authors..." (Karolides, 1992, p. 28). This traditional approach to literature is still widely-practiced today; it is the approach used in the teaching of English 3/American literature in the State of Florida, and it focuses on reading for test-taking purposes (MDCPS, 2012).

The end of World War I in 1918, however, ushered in an era of literary theory known as New Criticism. This theory refuted the significance of biographical and historical data to interpretive text analyses. Each piece was to be regarded as a single unit, and analyses focused on language aspects such as symbolic representations and visual descriptions. Conflicts were investigated as well and identified, and defined in psychological terms. As Christenbury explains, "Thus, New Criticism, ...was literature without the influence of the reader, the historical context, or the personal history of the author" (1992, p. 34). These analyses were achieved through a scrutinized reading, commonly referred to in the reading community as a close reading (Karolides, 1992), and this type of instructional approach to literature still has its followers.

Karolides discussed the elements of the traditional approaches to literature instruction:

Traditional approaches are based on several underlying assumptions: (a) the author's intention is the key to ascertaining what the work means and this meaning can be identified; (b) the text is an object that has a determinate meaning of its own; (c) the text can be analyzed through objective close scrutiny of its formal structure and techniques to establish the meaning. Furthermore, it is often assumed that there is but one meaning. In these approaches, the reader's role is neglected or omitted entirely. (1992, p. 28)

Consequently, the traditional approaches to the instruction of literature had similar foundations, but the angle of instruction differed. The "biographical-historical" (Karolides, 1992, p. 28) approach focused on the life and historical times of the author, including the predominant literary and social movements. The other approach, New Criticism, rejected all of the author-based information and the social factors. It focused entirely on the form and structure of the text; it was studying the text of the literature in isolation (1992).

Although pedagogical aspects of the two most widely-accepted traditional approaches to literature differ, an important theoretical aspect is quite similar. This is explained by the fact that in both instances, knowledge given to the reader, whether it is about the author and times as in the biographical/historical approach, or the content and form of the text as in New Criticism, is purportedly for the purpose of enhancing the reader's comprehension. However, the timing of this provision is problematic from the viewpoint of the transactional theory of literature as recommended by Rosenblatt (1938). This is because traditionally, the background knowledge is given before the student reads the piece of literature. This practice has "...the effect of derailing the reader's transaction with the text and denying the opportunity to attend to and develop that experience" (Karolides, 1992, p. 29).

The elements of Rosenblatt's transactional theory of literature, (and its possible benefits for literature instruction), became available to the literary community in 1938 with the publication of her first book. However, the traditional approaches to literature instruction had become anchored in America's literary pedagogy and were the accepted norm, almost to the exclusion of all others, until the late 1960s. That particular time period however, mirrored nation-wide unrest. This was fueled by our country's reactions to the Vietnam War and was exemplified by Americans' desire for social change. Civil groups in favor of social justice became more organized and powerful. There was friction and unrest as the Civil Rights Movement, the Feminist Movement, and the Peace Movement achieved their voices. Often during these turbulent times, these movements sounded as one voice which generated a social power that was quite unlike any other voice since our nation's creation (Spring, 1997). As a logical result, objections to the existing sterile approach to literature were being heard in the university communities across the nation, and new, different, and previously ignored approaches to literature were finally given a chance (Rosenblatt, 1995). The affective nature of personal responses to literature, which encourage and elicit varied meanings of texts, was a particular inducement to many educators at this time. Rosenblatt's theory had gained attention at all levels of schooling, elementary, secondary, and postsecondary. Times were changing and the voices of students as readers were given power (Luke, 2012). As Willinsky (1990) stipulated about reader response, "In more general terms, literature becomes a means for the moral and intellectual construction of the self" (as cited in Luke, 2012). The instruction in literature classes for many students had changed considerably.

Unfortunately, the momentum of reader response acceptance was significantly hindered as an effect of the push towards high-stakes standardized testing. Efferent reading, reading to carry away information for the purpose of answering test questions, is the modern-day version of the traditional approaches to literature that were strict, formal, and objective (Iser, 1971). For the most part, today's readers are denied the opportunity to engage with the text and experience the text from their own perspectives. Rosenblatt's reader response theory (1938, 1995), which emphasized the reader's transaction with the text was out-of-sync with the high-stakes testing movement. The political forces governing the curriculum have failed to recognize, or have chosen to overlook, the possible positive effects of authentic use of print activities like reader response on students.

Several basic concepts form the foundation of Rosenblatt's idea of reader response. Foremost in her theory was the notion that anything and everything that can be experienced in life can be found in literature; literature offers the whole range of all things that can be classified as human. She reminded us that literature also carries or offers both implicit and explicit values, and that those values are of every conceivable kind: moral, social, behavioral and psychological. She suggested that because of the fact that values are in literature, teachers must be constantly aware of the wide scope of implied generalizations that literature makes about humans, human nature, and society. Each piece of literature, therefore, offers either implicitly or explicitly, the views and generalizations that come from the mind, or minds, of the author or authors. Teachers must also be cognizant of their own preconceived notions about humans and human nature, and most importantly, according to Rosenblatt, they must constantly remember that each person finds a piece of literature understandable, (or not), based on *their own understandings* of humans, human nature, and society. Individuals cannot escape the guiding and forming influence of the culture into which they were born, therefore, humans are constantly comparing, contrasting, and measuring human nature to that which has been experienced (Rosenblatt, 1995). She did not separate the reader from the text, as she explained in the following:

> In the past, reading has too often been thought of as an interaction, the printed page impressing its meaning on the reader's mind or the reader extracting the meaning embedded in the text. Actually, reading is a constructive, selective process over time in a particular context. The relation between reader and signs on the page proceeds in a to-and-fro spiral, in which each is continually being affected by what the other has contributed. (p. 26)

Rosenblatt (1995) described a dynamic and personal interchange that she labeled the transaction between the reader and the text. To participate in this ongoing negotiation and collaboration and create meaning, the reader must draw from his/her prior knowledge, or lived experiences. There is no meaning without the reader's transaction with the text; there is simply a sequence of visual signs on a page. If the literature is voiced and therefore audible, then without the transaction only verbal signs exist. This transaction is influenced by the reader's motivations or his/her purpose or purposes for engaging the text, identified by Rosenblatt as the reader's stance (Rosenblatt, 1995). She explained the reader's stance as a continuum ranging "…from predominantly nonliterary, or, to use my terminology, efferent reading, to predominantly literary, or aesthetic, reading" (1995, p. 292). *Oxford Dictionaries Online* (2012) defines the adjective efferent as coming from the mid 19th century Latin verb *efferre,* which is a combination of *ex*, meaning out and *ferre*, meaning *carry*. Rosenblatt used this term for reading to *carry away information.* In the language of today's curriculum, this is reading to find answers to factual questions; it is the type of reading that is required of students on assessment tests. This is efferent reading because it "…requires attention mainly to the public aspects of meaning and excludes, pushes into the periphery, personal feelings or ideas activated" (1995, p. 292). Conversely, aesthetic reading calls to consciousness a mix of public links to the words and the personal transaction with the text that includes the reader's unique blend of lived experiences, emotions, and concepts. The reader's attention is centered on what he/she is living through, experiencing, throughout the actual reading event (Rosenblatt, 1995).

Today's adolescents, products of schooled literacy and the banking concept of education and victims of the high-stakes testing movement, are aware that the assessment tests that they will be required to take will focus on factual questions. They have been practicing this efferent reading since their initial reading experiences when they were asked, "What is the main idea of this story?" Their personal feelings and cultural identities have been marginalized; most of them have been deprived of experiencing aesthetic reading transactions with the text (Rosenblatt, 1995). This study promoted the aesthetic reading experience by implementing the use of Rosenblatt's reader response theory which emphasized each reader's unique transactions with the text (Rosenblatt, 1995).

High School Juniors, English 3, and Self-Efficacy Beliefs

Many juniors struggle with the English 3 curriculum. For those who have not passed the 10th grade state reading comprehension test, the pressure of passing English 3 can be overwhelming. The construct of self-efficacy beliefs can play an elemental part in an individual student's likelihood of succeeding in this academic domain.

Albert Bandura's, *Social Foundations of Thought and Action*, (1986) described "...a theoretical framework for analyzing human motivation, thought, and action from a social cognitive perspective" (p.xi). He called this framework social cognitive theory. Although many people and theorists refer to social cognitive theory "...as social learning theory" (p. xi) this label is not accurate. Social learning theory refers to "...the concept of learning as a conditioning model of response acquisition" (p. xii), but for social cognitive theorists, "...learning is conceptualized mainly as knowledge acquisition through cognitive processing of information" (p. xii). This theoretical difference made social cognitive theory a more accurate description.

Bandura's (1986) social cognitive theory was based on the concept of reciprocal determinism..." or "...reciprocal causation" (p. xi). This concept is composed of three elements and is "...an interactional model of causation in which environmental events, personal factors, and behavior all operate as interacting determinants of each other" (p.xi). Within this model, for perhaps the first time, individuals are seen to have an amount of control over their actions, destinies, and self-directions (1986). Other theories have emphasized the social origins of thought, but this theory with its representative model of causation embraced the inquiry into the "mechanisms of performances" (Bandura,1986, p. xi). Social cognitive theory examines "...the processes by which people regulate their behavior through internal standards and self-evaluative reactions to their own behavior" (1986, p. 390). Bandura argued, however, that self-efficacy has the greatest influence on people's lives of the many components involved in individuals' systems of self-knowledge (1986) , and he defines self-efficacy beliefs as "people's judgments of their capabilities to organize and execute courses of action required to attain designated types of performances" (1986, p. 391). This is because self-efficacy beliefs are perceived capabilities not only to produce results but to attain wanted results. This is an important deviation from other concepts of competence because self-efficacy beliefs are specific to a task and a situation; they are contextual in nature (Bandura, 1986; Pintrich & Schunk, 1995).

Self-efficacy beliefs are also sensitive to the regulation of other factors. When faced with something that requires an individual to take action, changes in such things as motivation, thoughts, feelings, and the environment may be perceived as necessary. When this occurs, self-efficacy beliefs can be influenced by these changes (Pajares, 1997). The converse of this phenomenon is also true because Bandura (1982, 1997), Schunk (2004) and Schunk & Pajares (1995) found that thinking, feeling, acting, and motivating are greatly influenced by self-efficacy beliefs. These beliefs are not to be mistaken for an individual's feeling of knowing what to do.

37

Rather, an individual's self-efficacy beliefs are concerned with that person's concept of believing that he/she is capable of accomplishing a particular task at a particular level. It is not the question of possessing certain skills; it is the profound opinion of what can be achieved by a person with his/her particular skills. Further, it has been found that the influence of self-efficacy beliefs extends to multiple areas of a person's life: task choice, effort, motivation, persistence, resilience, and achievement (Bandura, 1982, 1997; Schunk, 2004; Schunk, & Pajares, 1995).

Research has also been done regarding the possibility that there are differences in self-efficacy beliefs between male and female study participants. Pajares and Johnson (1996) and Pajares and Miller (1994, 1995) found that girls and boys performed academic tasks with equal capability. These studies, however, also revealed that even though the academic performance of the girls was equal to the academic performance of the boys, the girls reported lower levels of self-efficacy beliefs regarding the academic tasks (1994, 1995, 1996). Differences in levels of self-efficacy between sexes were also reported by Tomte and Hatlevik (2011). This study involved self-efficacy, Information and Communication Technology (ICT) user profiles, and sex. Positive relationships were found regarding both sexes, but the self-efficacy levels of males and females were not the same, even when the user profiles were identical (2011).

Self-efficacy is believed to have two aspects, it is predictive in nature because an individual formulates self-efficacy beliefs before becoming engaged in a task, and because it exists as a perception, its accuracy may be questionable (Bandura, 1982, 1997; Schunk, 2004; Schunk & Pajares, 1995). Some studies (Bandura, 1997; Lane & Lane, 2004; Linnenbrink & Pintrich, 2003; Schunk, 1989; Zimmerman, 2000) provide compelling evidence that supports the role of self-efficacy on performance to be influential, even though it may act as an indirect mediator. The relationship of students' self-efficacy to their engagement in a task is a strong one. Besides the quantity of effort, the quality of effort in terms of deeper processing strategies and a general cognitive engagement of learning have been strongly linked to self-efficacy perceptions (Linnenbrink & Pintrich, 2003).

Studies indicate that higher self-efficacy beliefs result in a longer period of engagement. Moreover, the longer task engagement results in higher achievement, and this higher achievement, or mastery experience, is an extremely powerful source of self-efficacy (Bandura, 1982, 1986, 1994, 1997). Although high self-efficacy beliefs cannot compensate for a lack of ability, a person with high self-efficacy beliefs but low ability will perform better than a person of the same ability who has low self-efficacy beliefs. However, this individual will not outperform an individual with high self-efficacy beliefs and high ability for that particular task (Bandura, 1977, 1982, 1986, 1994, 1997).

Pintrich and Schunk (2002) discussed the relationship of self-efficacy beliefs to motivation, which is defined as "the process whereby goal-directed behavior is instigated and sustained" (p. 5). Self-efficacy is believed to act as a mediator between motivation and task achievement, with highly-efficacious students being more likely to persist on a task and engage sophisticated ways of learning than students with lower-self-efficacy, resulting in higher achievement levels that expected (Linnenbrink & Pintrich, 2003). In addition, Pajares addressed the validity of Bandura's theoretical representation of self-efficacy beliefs, "...the self-efficacy construct is embedded in a theory of human social cognition, whereas most expectancy constructs that can presently be found in the literature offer few theoretical underpinnings or connections to broader theoretical tenets" (1997). Finally, the studies of Alvermann (2001, 2003), Kamil et al., (2000) have confirmed that adolescent learners with high self-efficacy, the knowledge that they are capable of succeeding at a task, are more likely to do school-related reading than those who lack this confidence. In addition, Guthrie and Wigfield (2000) emphasized the importance of student self-efficacy beliefs and student engagement to effective literacy instruction.

The implications of these studies are of particular importance to high school students who must achieve credits in mandatory subjects. Implementing the aesthetic reading of American literature and the reading strategy of transactional reader response could very possibly enhance the self-efficacy beliefs of English 3 students as they consider their likelihood of academic success. In Florida, the implications are particularly weighty for juniors; they are mandated by law to take and pass English 3 in order to graduate (Florida Department of Education, 2012b).

In this study, the intervention consisted of aesthetic reading of English 3 literature in place of the advocated efferent reading. Through the strategy of reader response, the predominantly Hispanic student population of the experimental group was encouraged to respond personally, culturally, and experientially to the literature. The encouragement and acceptance of students' personal responses to literature as they read aesthetically was intended to support students' personal connections. Giving students high-level academic credit for completing their reader responses and showing that their responses connected to the text in some way represented a form of mastery experience, (of comprehending the literature from their own perspectives). Research has indicated that mastery experience strengthens self-efficacy beliefs (Bandura, 1982, 1986; 1994, 1997).

Summary

Education, politics and governmental policies have been intricately intertwined since America's inception as a republic (Spring, 1997). Presently, however, the various state and federal legislations, NCLB (U. S. Department of Education, 2002), RTTP (U. S. Department of Education, 2009), and the Common Core Standards Initiative (NGACBP & CCSSO, 2010), have forced the nation's education system into an unprecedented time of high-stakes testing and accountability.

State and governmental legislative acts have caused Florida's ELAR teachers to be focused on their students' scores on the standardized state tests in reading comprehension and writing, known as the FCAT (Florida Department of Education, 2012a). The secondary English curriculum has changed throughout history to accommodate the various social and political climates of the times (Applebee, 1974; Spring, 1997). Over the last three decades, it has accommodated the push for data-driven accountability by increasingly emphasizing reading for test-taking and test preparation, (efferent reading); reading for personal enjoyment and personal relevancy, (aesthetic reading) have both become secondary (MDCPS, 2012). The students who do not succeed with the reading tests often display problems with the efferent reading strategies that are used to help them and often have trouble succeeding in their English 3/American literature class (Florida Department of Education, 2012c).

Self-efficacy beliefs, which form an intricate part of a person's self-knowledge, are perceived self-judgments that individuals make about their capacity to not only produce results but to attain wanted results (Bandura, 1986, 1994, 1997). Research studies (Bandura, 1986; Pintrich & Schunk, 1995) have indicated that these beliefs are both task and situation specific and therefore, contextual in nature. An individual's self-efficacy beliefs also influence other areas of that person's life such as: task choice, effort, motivation, persistence, resilience, and achievement (Bandura, 1982, 1997; Schunk, 2004; Schunk & Pajares, 1995). This influence specifically extends to academic achievement as Alvermann (2001, 2003) and Kamil et al (2000) have indicated that if an individual's reading-related self-efficacy beliefs have been lowered, success in other academic domains like math and writing can be more difficult to attain (Alvermann, 2001, 2003).

Although a review of the research revealed some studies that involved reading self-efficacy beliefs, reading strategies, and reading comprehension (Bandura & Schunk, 1981; McCabe et al., 2006; McCrudden et al., 2005; Naseri, 2012; Nelson & Manset-Williamson, 2006; Van Keer & Verhaeghe, 2005;), gaps were found in the literature. Specific research gaps were evident in areas that would have been crucial to this study: high school students and any type of reader response, high school students and their elf-efficacy beliefs about reading comprehension, the effects on students' self-efficacy beliefs, any age or educational level, when students aesthetically read fictive and nonfictive texts, and responded to these texts with aesthetically-evoked reader responses, as well as any research regarding English 3/American literature students.

This study was undertaken to find evidence in support of the belief that literacy acquisition must be perceived from an individualized engagement with the text, and that this type of authentic use of print activity can increase students' self-efficacy beliefs about their reading comprehension of American literature. This study took place in a large Title 1 magnet high school and addressed the research gaps by:

1. randomly-selecting a control group and an experimental group from a population of regular-level English 3/American literature classes
2. pre- and post-testing both groups about their self-efficacy beliefs regarding their comprehension of American literature.
3. maintaining the same text selections for both groups during the study period.
4. substituting aesthetic reading for efferent reading in the experimental group.
5. substituting aesthetically-evoked reader responses for the curriculum-mandated activities in the experimental group.
6. maintaining the curriculum-mandated activities in the control group.

The chapter that follows will describe the methods undertaken to determine the effect of the treatment intervention and to address the previously mentioned gaps in the research literature.

CHAPTER III

METHODS

The purpose of this chapter is to describe the research methods that were used in this study. The participants in this study were students who were enrolled in regular English 3/American literature classes. This chapter discusses the following components of this study: design, participants, setting, procedures, research measures, research questions, and data analyses.

Design

This study used a quasi-experimental pretest-posttest design to measure the effects of the two-step strategy of aesthetic reading and reader response, implemented as one intervention, on students' self-efficacy beliefs regarding their comprehension of American literature and success in English 3. The treatment and control groups for this study were picked from a convenience sample of six regular English 3 classrooms in an urban high school in Florida. There was, however, random assignment to treatment group.

Participants

The participants of this study were students who were registered in regular English 3 classes at a large Title I magnet high school that is located in the largest school district in the State of Florida. As in recent years, the school's population was predominantly Hispanic; percentages of other races/ethnicities were also represented and the study's sample reflected this. The student population was: 14% White, Non-Hispanic, 21% Black, Non-Hispanic, 64% Hispanic, and 2% Asian/Indian/Multiracial (Florida Department of Education, 2013b). The percentage of students who received free/reduced lunch was similar to the previous year, 79% (Florida Department of Education, 2013a). As with all other schools in Florida, the site school has been graded since 1999. The average grade over the 14 years has been a D, although the school received a C for the 2011-2012 school year. The factors used by the State of Florida to figure the school grades for high schools were changed again for the 2012-2013 school year; this caused the school grades to be delayed. However, these grades were finally published this spring, 2014; the site school received another C (Florida Department of Education, 2013c).

Setting

Passing English 3/American literature is required for graduation in the State of Florida (Florida Department of Education, 2012b). The site school offered several English classes that fulfilled this requirement for 11th graders: Exceptional Student Education English 3, regular English 3, regular/inclusion English 3, English 3

Honors, Advanced Placement (AP) English, and 11th grade English for the International Baccalaureate (IB) Program. The study took place in classes that were designated as regular. These classes were comprised of students whose previous academic performance in English had been determined to be at an average level by their academic counselors. At the site school, the vast majority of students in regular English 3 classes had not passed the 10th grade FCAT reading test. Students who had been determined to be of regular level, but who had formerly been in Exceptional Student Education classes for English were placed in regular/inclusion English classes where they benefitted from the presence of a second teacher who was certified in Exceptional Education. For the most part, students who had passed the 10th grade FCAT reading test were placed in the higher level English classes, such as English 3 Honors or AP classes. The students who were accepted into the IB Program were required to take the 11th grade IB English classes; they were not enrolled in the classes that were part of the regular English curriculum. All classes met every other school day for 90 minutes, and all of the classes were coeducational.

Procedures

Preparations for this study at the school site were initiated during the grading period previous to the planned study time. These preparations involved a series of three workshops that were conducted by the researcher for the purpose of informing and instructing interested English department members about aesthetic reading and aesthetically-evoked reader responses and the forthcoming study. The workshops were held after the regular department meetings and were open to other faculty members and administrators. Different members of the English department attended different workshops; however, three English 3/American literature teachers expressed interest in being part of the study and were present for all three workshops.

The first teacher workshop consisted of a presentation of the study. The following components were explained: the problem, the purpose, the general theories involved, and the timeline. The consent forms and the demographic survey were shown and explained, as well as the procedures to guarantee student anonymity and privacy. The pretest/posttest instrument for measuring the students' self-efficacy beliefs regarding their comprehension of American literature, the modified Confidence in Reading American Literature Survey (CRAL; see Appendix D) was presented and explained.

The second workshop was an intense explanation of aesthetic reading of literature and reader response theory as defined by Louise Rosenblatt (1938, 1978, 1995, 2003). The researcher provided an explanation of student self-efficacy as it pertained to the study, and explained and modeled the differences between efferent reading and aesthetic reading of literature during this workshop. Literature selections

43

from the English 3/American literature textbook, (those not mandated for use during the school year), were used. Examples of other familiar literature pieces were also taken from a college textbook that is used to teach teachers about aesthetic reading and responding, *Reader Response in the Classroom: Evoking and Interpreting Meaning in Literature*, edited by the well-known reader response expert, Nicholas J. Karolides and published in 1992. Copies of the format for the reader response journal, a form of two-column notes, (see Appendix F) was distributed to the teachers, as well as the reader response starters (see Appendix I). Aesthetic reading of literature excerpts, followed by aesthetically-evoked reader responses in the form of two-column notes was modeled for the teachers at this time. A question/answer/discussion session followed, giving the teachers an opportunity to gain clarification about aesthetic reading and reader response. A number of questions were asked, and the attendees seemed content with the answers that were given.

The third workshop had several purposes. Teachers practiced aesthetic reading and reader response using the response starters if they wanted to, and this practice was followed by a sharing and discussing session. This session also included an explanation and short practice session about using the simple rubric (see Appendix G) provided for rating the reader responses. This rubric offers teachers a method of evaluating the reader responses for the purpose of awarding letter grades. Examples of aesthetically-invoked responses were demonstrated as well as the use of sample comments that provided students with positive feedback about their reader responses (see Appendix H). It was explained that such comments may be necessary to build students' confidence about their own connections to the text. This is because the majority of the reading that students have experienced in school is efferent and has concentrated on finding information that provides them with information that they need to for answering multiple choice-type questions. It was explained that students may be perplexed about the acceptability of writing about their own transactions with the texts at first and may need reassurance; the positive feedback comments (see Appendix H) were developed by the researcher solely for the convenience of the teacher. Teachers would be free to use their own positive comments. The timeline of the study was explained, including the alignment of the study's literature selections with the District's Pacing Guide (MDCPS, 2012) which designated the assignments and instructional objectives for each of the weeks during the study. The procedures for the experimental classes were made clear, both verbally and in written form; it was also explained that the control class teachers would simply instruct their classes as they normally would, following the District's Pacing Guide (MDCPS, 2012). An important point of this workshop was to reinforce the fact that the study's intervention was only to be used in the experimental classes. As the study was planned for the following grading period, the number of classes and teachers that would be able to participate was unknown at the time of the last workshop.

The study was to begin during the first nine weeks of the 2013-2014 school year. At the very beginning of the nine weeks, the researcher discovered that only one of the three English 3/American literature teachers that had expressed their desire to participate in the study would be still assigned to teach those classes. The other two teachers had experienced changes to their teaching assignments. This resulted in a difference in the availability of classes for the study. There were only six English 3 regular classes available, and all six of these classes were assigned to one teacher, who expressed the desire to participate in the study. This teacher had attended the workshops, and therefore was knowledgeable about the study. From the six available classes, four classes for the study were determined by using a random number generator. A coin flip was used to determine the two classes that were assigned to the treatment group and the two classes that were assigned to the control (Malo-Juvera, 2012). This process resulted in periods one and two being assigned to the control group, and periods three and five were in the treatment group. Each of the classes was comprised of no more than 25 students.

Teacher and Researcher

This study was conducted at the school site by a teacher and the researcher, who is also a certified teacher. At the beginning of the school year the school site principal had suggested that the teacher, (see below), instruct the control classes and the researcher (see below), instruct the intervention classes. This request was made because the principal had been notified that the site school's standardized state test scores were indicating that the school would fall a letter grade; the school had therefore been targeted for multiple district, county, and state visits during the first several months of the school year, until at least December, when the official State of Florida School Grades (Florida Department of Education, 2013c) for high schools, were expected to be finalized and published. The principal had surmised that although the research study had been approved by the county, placing the researcher as the instructor for the intervention classes provided the placement of the teacher as the instructor for the control classes. These placements successfully eliminated the necessity of the administration having to explain, (repeatedly, because of the expected bi- or tri-weekly visits), why the regular, contracted teacher was not instructing according to the District Pacing Guide for English 3 regular classes (MDCPS, 2012). The researcher had retired from teaching, (from the county and therefore, from the school site), at the end of August, 2013. The teacher and the researcher readily agreed to comply with the principal's request and were grateful for the principal's high degree of support for the study and for his professionalism.

45

The teacher and researcher who participated in the study were certified high school teachers who have taught a variety of high school courses and grade levels. The teacher holds a Professional Certificate in English, Grades 6-12. She has a Master's degree in English Education and has taught for six years, with the last four years at the site school. The researcher holds a Professional Certificate in English, Grades 6-12, a Professional Middle Grades Endorsement, and a Professional Certificate in Reading, (grades K-12). Her M. S. degree is in Reading, and she has recently retired from teaching at the site school, (the last 16 years of her 37 years of teaching).

Informed Consent and Assent

Parental consent forms and student assent forms were required for this study. The parent consent form (see Appendix A) and the student assent form (see Appendix B) were given to the participants of the treatment and control groups to be completed at home. Both of the forms were distributed the week before the study began. Each form explained that the purpose of the study was to examine the effects of a particular approach to reading and responding to American literature, aesthetic reading and reader response, on students' self-efficacy beliefs about their abilities to comprehend and succeed in English 3/American literature.

Both the parental consent form and the student assent form explained several other features of the study. These features included the information that the study would use the required English 3 curriculum textbook and the literature selections from the instructional guides that Miami-Dade County Public Schools requires (Miami-Dade County Public Schools, 2012). As was explained in the consent form and assent form, only students who had returned completed consent and assent forms were allowed to participate in the study. Both of the forms explained that the participants' privacy would be protected, and this was accomplished by the use of anonymous inventories. This anonymity was guaranteed in two ways. Participants used the last five digits of their seven-digit student identification number on the pretest and posttest inventories, and the original inventories were destroyed after the information was entered into the statistical software (Malo-Juvera, 2012).

Pilot Test of Survey

A pilot test of the Confidence in Reading American Literature (CRAL) Survey (see Appendix D) was run several days before the actual study time. The participants were enrolled in another regular English 3 class at the site school, but they were not enrolled in any of the classes that were involved in either the control group or the treatment group of the study. The survey was given for several purposes: to make sure the directions and questions were very clear, to make sure the answer choices were clear, and to see if any of the questions posed any type of concern for any of the students. The results of this procedure indicated that there were no foreseeable issues with administering the survey.

Demographic Survey, Pretest and Posttest Inventories

At the beginning of the first class of the study, a short demographic survey (see Appendix C) and the pretest inventory (see Appendix D) were completed by all participants. Both the survey and the pretest inventory were completed anonymously, which was accomplished, as was previously mentioned, by requiring only the last five digits of each participant's seven-digit student identification number on both the demographic survey and pretest inventory (Malo-Juvera, 2012).

The privacy procedure described for the demographic survey and the pretest inventory was repeated during the final class of the study, class eight, when the participants completed the posttest inventory. This procedure allowed for the correct matching of the demographic survey, the pretest inventory, and the posttest inventory of each participant without compromising the participants' privacy. As has been mentioned, to further guarantee the participants' anonymity, the original inventories were destroyed when all of the data were entered into the statistical software (Malo-Juvera, 2012).

Rationale for Time Allotted

The amount of time for this proposed study was determined from a review of the available research; however, this search revealed a void of studies regarding the effects of reading strategies on high school students' self-efficacy beliefs. Several studies (Bandura & Schunk, 1981; McCrudden et al., 2005; Nelson & Manset-Williamson, 2006; Van Keer & Verhaeghe, 2005) were found that involved the effects of instructional strategies on elementary students, and two other studies that were found (McCabe et al., 2006; Naseri, 2012) targeted college students.

The studies with elementary school participants provided part of the foundation and support for determining the appropriate amount of time required for the proposed study. Bandura and Schunk (1981) studied elementary children who had severe math deficits and the effects of an instructional program that involved either subgoals that were easily attainable, goals that were more comprehensive and thus more difficult to attain, or no goals at all. That study looked at the participants' cultivation of competencies, their self-efficacy beliefs, and their intrinsic interest; the study period was seven, 30 minute sessions in a regular elementary learning environment. A second elementary study by McCrudden et al., (2005) took place during five sessions in a regular elementary learning environment on five different days, and occurred over a time period of two weeks. That study looked at fifth graders' self-efficacy and interest in the use of reading strategies. In a third elementary study, Nelson and

47

Manset-Williamson (2006) looked at explicit versus less-explicit reading strategy instruction, self-efficacy beliefs and several other factors. The participants were fourth-eighth graders, and the intervention was implemented four times per week over a five week time period. Finally, a long term elementary study (Van Keer & Verhaeghe, 2005), took place over a year and involved second and fifth graders and studied the effects of reading strategy instruction and peer-tutoring on self-efficacy beliefs as well as other factors.

Support for the time allotted for this study also came from some studies with college students. Naseri (2012) found significant positive correlations between reading self-efficacy beliefs and reading comprehension, as well as reading self-efficacy beliefs and reading strategy use. His study took place during one college class period. Additionally, McCabe et al., (2006) studied the effects of various text formats on students' self-efficacy beliefs about reading; they also studied the effects on students' subsequent reading comprehension. The participants were underachieving first-year college students, and that study took place over two college classes that were about a month apart.

The participants of this study were high school juniors who were neither elementary nor college students like the participants in the studies found in the literature. The average age of a high school junior falls between the age groups used in those previous research studies, their school and learning environments were quite different from both elementary and college students' environments, and their academic and social priorities differed as well. The differences in ages and learning environments were taken into consideration, as well as the study similarities of topic and purpose to determine the appropriate length of the proposed study. The research studies that involved college students were given more consideration in regard to the amount of time needed than the elementary studies because the high school juniors were closer in age and maturity to college students than they were to elementary students. High school students also attended classes according to a designated schedule and were usually with a different mix of students in each class; this was more similar to an average college freshman's schedule than it was to an elementary student's schedule. All of these factors were used to determine that the eight-class time period of the study. This eight-class time period translated into three weeks because the study conformed to the site school's block scheduling; classes met every other school day for 90 minutes.

Class Procedures

The study began in the fifth week of school according to the district school calendar. For this study, the control group's teacher followed the District Pacing Guide for English 3 regular classes (MDCPS, 2012), which provided the approximate timeline, instructional goals, and recommended texts for each week of the school year. At the request of the principal, both the experimental and control classes followed the district's text recommendations during the study's time period. The experimental classes, however, used the study's two-part intervention of aesthetic reading and writing aesthetically-evoked reader responses in place of the district's recommended assignments.

Thus, the literature assignments for the intervention and control classes were the same assignments designated for the fifth, sixth, and seventh weeks of school in the District Pacing Guide (MDCPS, 2012). The control classes were taught in the standard, efferent-based manner. The intervention classes, though, received different instruction; practice and instruction on both aesthetic reading and writing aesthetically-evoked reader responses was given. Led by the researcher, the intervention classes were given time to practice the following on the first two days of the study: aesthetic reading, writing aesthetically-evoked responses, reading the teacher's comments regarding their responses, asking for help and guidance, as well as rewriting their practice responses if they chose to do so.

Following the practice session, the intervention classes moved on to the regular literature selections. They were reminded to read the assignments aesthetically, paying attention to their thoughts, connections, remembrances, reactions, and feelings, (just as they had practiced). They wrote a required number of aesthetically-evoked reader responses using a two-column format (see Appendix F) for each text assignment. The left-hand column of the reader response page designated the pages and the quotes of the student's choice. The number of responses required was assigned according to the study's protocol (see Tables 1-7). In the right-hand column the student wrote his/her aesthetically-evoked response for each quote. The researcher gave the experimental classes specific directions regarding the reading and response assignments before the study began, and the number of responses required from each student per assignment was also stipulated at the time the assignment was given.

In the intervention classes, the reader response journals were reviewed by the researcher 10 times during the study's duration of eight classes. The researcher's review process followed the provided rubric (see Appendix G). The rubric outlined the grading procedure which included a way to evaluate completion, (which differed with each assignment and was based on the number of quotes required for each text selection). The evaluation protocol for the reader responses also stipulated that each response had to be reviewed to make sure that each one revealed some sort of connection to the quote that the student chose or to the text in general. The grading protocol had been explained to the classes prior to the random determination of which classes would be in the control group and the treatment group, as well as before any consent or assent forms were distributed. Therefore, the students in the treatment group knew that a letter grade would be given for each assignment before they gave their assent to be in the study. They also were aware of the aforementioned grading requirements. The researcher also provided comments on each assignment (see Appendix H). Suggested comments were simply a positive word or phrase to motivate each student, letting them know that their responses, (or attempts to respond) were valid. As it took some students longer than others to respond with confidence, suggestions to encourage this were sometimes included. There were no correct or incorrect responses to the text because students were responding to what they read as individuals; any type of logical response that expressed the student's connection to the quote was considered acceptable (Rosenblatt, 1938, 1978, 1995, 2003).

The researcher, as the teacher in the intervention classroom, followed the study's timetable for aesthetic reading and response assignments during the study's timeframe of eight classes, or approximately three weeks. Most of the assignments came from the designated textbook for English 3, *Literature: American Literature* (McDougal Littell, 2012). Please (see Tables 1-7) for assignment information. Several assignments came from the section of the District's Pacing Guide that was labeled as appropriate outside texts (MDCPS, 2012).

Table 1

Assignments for Class 1 and Class 2

Classes of Study	Assignment/Author/Page
1 & 2	from *Call of the Wild* by Jack London

Procedures

Class 1 and Class 2

(1) demographic survey and CRAL inventory (pretest) (see Appendix D)

(2) researcher modeled aesthetic reading and writing of a reader response using an excerpt from *Call of the Wild* by Jack London and suggested response starters

(3) student questions and discussion/explanation/review

(4) students were given a copy of the response starters (to use if they wish) and a two-column reader response sheet

(5) students practiced reading aesthetically and writing a minimum of four aesthetically-evoked responses on their own, using another part of the excerpt.

(6) reader responses were collected and reviewed by the teacher for the next class

(7) researcher utilized the rubric (see Appendix G) for rating/grading and applicable comments (see Appendix H)

Table 2

Assignments for Class 3

Classes of Study	Assignment/Author/Page
3	"I Hear America Singing" by Walt Whitman" (508-510)

Procedures

Class 3

(1) researcher returned the practice responses from Class 2

(2) researcher walked around, offered assistance & explained comments

(3) students read more of the excerpt (individually) and were assigned 2 more responses, paying attention to the comments they had been given on the last assignment

(4) researcher walked around and wrote comments on the new responses/offered assistance as requested or needed

(5) response sheets and excerpts collected

(6) new response sheets distributed

(7) introduction to the author (see page 508)

(8) review of literary terms: free verse, cataloging, repetition, parallelism, and tone (see page 509)

(9) summative review of the aesthetic reading process

10) independent & aesthetic reading of "I Hear America Singing" by Walt Whitman (see page 510)

(11) students were assigned a minimum of four aesthetically-evoked reader responses-(researcher paid attention to students who signaled her for help)*

(12) responses collected

(13) researcher rated/graded the responses (see Appendix G), added positive, encouraging comments (see Appendix H)

* students who had difficulty with the aesthetically-evoked responses were reminded of suggested response starters (See Appendix I)

Table 3

Assignments for Class 4

	Assignment/Author/Page
<u>4</u>	"A Noiseless Patient Spider" and
	"Beat! Beat! Drums!" by Walt Whitman (516 &
	517)

Procedures

Class 4

(1) researcher returned the practice responses from Class 3

(2) researcher walked around, offered assistance & comment/grade explanations

(3) response sheets collected

(4) new response sheets distributed

(5) summative review of the aesthetic reading process

(6) independent & aesthetic reading of "Noiseless Patient Spider" by Walt Whitman

(see page 516)

(7) students were assigned a minimum of three aesthetically-evoked reader responses/

researcher paid attention to students who signaled her for help*

(8) independent & aesthetic reading of "Beat! Beat! Drums!" by Walt Whitman

(see page 517)

(9) students were assigned a minimum of four aesthetically-evoked reader responses;

researcher paid attention to students who signaled her for help)*

(10) reader responses were turned-in to the researcher for rating/grading (see Appendix G), comments/suggestions (see Appendix H)

*students who had having difficulty with the aesthetically-evoked responses were reminded of suggested response starters (See Appendix I)

Table 4

Assignments for Class 5

Classes of Study	Assignment/Author/Page
<u>5</u>	"Because I Could Not Stop for Death"
	by Emily Dickinson (526)

Procedures

<u>Class 5</u>

(1) researcher returned the practice responses from Class 4

(2) researcher walked around, offered assistance & comment/grade explanations

(3) response sheets collected

(4) new response sheets distributed

(5) summative review of the aesthetic reading process

(6) introduction to the author (see page 524)

(7) reviewed literary terms: quatrains, slant rhymes, figurative language, rhythm, and

imagery (see page 525)

(8) independent & aesthetic reading of "Because I Could Not Stop for Death" by

Emily Dickinson (see page 526)

(9) students were assigned a minimum of four aesthetically-evoked reader responses;

researcher paid attention to students who signaled her for help*

(10) **

(11) reader responses were turned-in to the researcher for rating (see Appendix G),
comments/suggestions (See Appendix H) and a grade

* students who had difficulty with the aesthetically-evoked responses were reminded of suggested
response starters (see Appendix I)

**regular level students traditionally have considerable difficulty with this poem-the remainder of
the class time was used to finish (10)

Table 5

Assignments for Class 6

Classes of Study	Assignment/Author/Page
<u>6</u>	"I Heard a Fly Buzz When I Died" by
	Emily Dickinson (531)

Procedures_____

Class 6

(1) researcher returned the responses from Class 5

(2) researcher walked around, offered assistance & comment/grade explanations

(3) response sheets collected

(4) new response sheets distributed

(5) summative review of the aesthetic reading process

(6) independent & aesthetic reading of "I Heard a Fly Buzz When I Died" by

Emily Dickinson (531)

(7) students were assigned a minimum of four aesthetically-evoked reader responses; researcher paid attention to students who signaled her for help*

(8) **

(9) reader responses were turned-in to the researcher for rating/grading (see

Appendix G), comments/suggestions (see Appendix H)

* students who had difficulty with the aesthetically-evoked responses were reminded of suggested response starters (see Appendix I)

**regular level students traditionally have considerable difficulty with this poem-the remainder of the class time was used to finish (7)

Table 6

Assignments of Class 7

Classes of Study	Assignment/Author/Page
<u>7</u>	*Uncle Tom's Cabin or Life Among the Lowly*
	by Harriet Beecher Stowe
	(Chapters 1 & 2)

Procedures

Class 7

(1) researcher returned the responses from Class 6

(2) researcher walked around, offered assistance & comment/grade explanations

Table 6 (continued)

Procedures for Class 7

(3) response sheets collected

(4) new response sheets distributed

(5) summative review of the aesthetic reading process

(6) independent & aesthetic reading of *Uncle Tom's Cabin or Life Among the Lowly*

by Harriet Beecher Stowe (Chapters 1 & 2)

(7) students were assigned a minimum of four aesthetically-evoked reader responses for

Chapter 1; 2 responses for Chapter 2; researcher paid attention to students

who signaled her for help

(8) reader responses were turned-in to the researcher for rating grading (see

Appendix G), comments/suggestions (see Appendix H)

* students who had having difficulty with the aesthetically-evoked responses were reminded of suggested response starters (see Appendix I)

Table 7

Assignments for Class 8

Classes of Study	Assignment/Author/Page
8	*Uncle Tom's Cabin or Life Among the Lowly* by Harriet Beecher Stowe, (Chapter 3)

Procedures

Class 8

(1) researcher returned the responses from Class 7

(2) researcher walked around, offered assistance & comment/grade explanations

(3) response sheets collected

(4) new response sheets distributed

(5) summative review of the aesthetic reading process

(6) independent & aesthetic reading of *Uncle Tom's Cabin or Life Among the Lowly*

by Harriet Beecher Stowe (Chapter 3)Table 7

Assignments for Class 8

(7) students were assigned a minimum of four aesthetically-evoked reader responses for

Chapter 3; researcher tended to students who signaled her for help*

(8) reader responses were turned-in to the researcher for rating/grading (see

Appendix G), comments/suggestions (see Appendix H)

(9) researcher explained that the responses from Class 8 would be returned to

them by their regular teacher after she graded them

(10) CRAL inventory (posttest) (see Appendix D)

* students who had difficulty with the aesthetically-evoked responses were reminded of suggested response starters (See Appendix I)

The assignments/procedures outlined above were covered in the intervention classes during the eight-class study period. Please note that during the first class of the study treatment, the students participated in a researcher-modeled practice session that introduced both aesthetic reading and the writing of aesthetically-evoked reader responses. An excerpt from the novel, *Call of the Wild* by Jack London (1915) was chosen by the researcher to model this practice session. Students had the opportunity to ask questions, and they were given the opportunity to read another part of the excerpt aesthetically and write four aesthetically-evoked reader responses in the two-column format (see Appendix F). To accommodate each unique class ethos, (the intervention group was comprised of two classes), as well as the researcher's discretion, during the eight-class time period the actual required time for the day's assignments fluctuated to a small degree. The overall schedule however, was maintained for the two classes that made-up the treatment group.

During the study's time period, the control groups were also instructed using the same text assignments as indicated in the District Pacing Guide (MDCPS, 2012), but the instruction did not include any part of the aesthetic reading and aesthetically-evoked reader response intervention. The regular teacher followed the designated curriculum with all of the classes once the study's time period was over.

Research Measures

This study utilized the Confidence in Reading American Literature (CRAL) Survey (see Appendix D) for the pretest and posttest. The researcher designed this survey to measure a student's perceived self-efficacy beliefs regarding the various tasks involved or relating to the specific domain of American literature comprehension. Bandura (2006) stated that "There is no all-purpose measure of perceived self-efficacy" (p. 307). This is because, as explained in his book, *Self-efficacy: The Exercise of Control* (1997) that to measure self-efficacy, the questions must be very specific to the actual task and functional domain that is being assessed and the levels of functioning must vary. Later, in 2006, Bandura reiterated that "Scales of perceived self-efficacy must be tailored to the particular domain of functioning that is the object of interest" (p. 307-308). Pajares (1997) added that "Researchers assess self-efficacy beliefs by asking individuals to report the level, generality, and strength of their confidence to accomplish a task and succeed in a certain situation" (p.7) and also that "...items [of self-efficacy assessments] should be worded in terms of can, a judgment of capability, rather than of will, a statement of intention" (p. 8). These criteria served as the developmental bases for the CRAL survey used in this study.

The study population's self-efficacy beliefs were measured by the CRAL survey both as the pretest and posttest. This instrument was developed specifically for students enrolled in regular English 3/American literature classes. It is therefore a modified version of the Self-Efficacy Beliefs in Reading (SER) scale (see Appendix E) created by Prat-Sala and Redford in 2010. The CRAL survey, like the SER, included the elements that both Bandura (1997, 2006) and Pajares (1997) had recommended for the creation of an appropriate and correct instrument for measuring self-efficacy beliefs. The reliability for the CRAL survey in this study met at least minimally acceptable standards (Fraenkel & Wallen, 2009); the Cronbach's alpha value for the pretest was .69 and the Cronbach's alpha for the posttest was .81.

Changes were made to the SER to meet both Bandura's (1997, 2006) and Pajares' (1997) recommendations. Still, the question stems on the CRAL were left the same as the original scale because they already satisfied the wording specification of using the term of "can" rather than "will" (Pajares, 1997). The specific domain of reading text selections in the American literature textbook replaced the original scale's domain, which pertained to reading for higher education classes and referred to journal articles and academic texts. The questions on the CRAL Survey, like the original, reflected various levels of cognitive functioning, which was determined by analyzing the questions from the perspective of *Bloom's Taxonomy of Educational Objectives, Handbook 1: The Cognitive Domain* (1956). Seaman's article, "Bloom's Taxonomy: Its Evolution, Revision, and Use in the Field of Education" (2011) offered support for the use of this taxonomy to analyze the inventory's questions; he discussed the history of educators' use of Bloom's taxonomy (1956) to analyze pedagogical materials since its inception. Pogrow (1993) talked about the use of this taxonomy during a research project at the University of Arizona wherein curricular materials for middle schools were evaluated for the purpose of ranking; the level of rigor was one of the criteria. McBain's (2011) classroom study supported the application of Bloom's taxonomy (1956) in determining the cognitive levels of materials and students' levels of functioning. The purpose of McBain's research was to try to help students understand higher-order thinking skills. Finally, Luebke and Lorie's (2013) article, "Use of Bloom's Taxonomy in Developing Reading Comprehension Specifications" found that the use of Bloom's taxonomy in the development of reading comprehension questions was effective in achieving testing goals. The task involved writing questions to meet the new design specifications for the law school entrance test that were based on levels of thinking/learning.

Supported by the aforementioned research, the process of using Bloom's taxonomy to analyze the questions of the CRAL exemplified the pedagogical analyses that educators have been performing for at least two decades, since the 1990s (Luebke & Lorie, 2013; McBain, 2011; Pogrow, 1993; Seaman, 2011). The procedures were comprised of reading each question on the survey and determining what level(s) of thinking/learning a student would need to be able to complete the question's task. These analyses revealed that the questions covered all of Bloom's six levels of thinking/learning: (a) knowledge (the most simplistic), (b) comprehension, (c) application, (d) analysis, (e) synthesis, and (f) evaluation (the highest and most complex level). These analyzes confirmed that the questions reflected varying levels of functioning; the CRAL met this criterion (Bandura, 1997). Additionally, unlike the original scale which used a seven-point Likert scale, the CRAL used a four-point Likert scale ranging from *1= not well at all* to *4= very well* to better accommodate the regular English 3/American literature students' comprehension levels. The four-point Likert format allowed the respondent to indicate "level, strength, and generality" (Pajares, 1997, p. 7) in their answer. The responses were positively loaded and a higher score was indicative of higher levels of self-efficacy beliefs.

Participants were directed to refrain from putting their names on the pretest/posttest inventory, the CRAL (see Appendix D), to protect their privacy. On both the short demographic survey that the participants completed on the first day of the study and on the pretest and posttest inventories, participants were instructed to put only the last five digits of their seven-digit student identification number for matching purposes only. With both the demographic questionnaire and the pretest and posttest inventories, the teacher/researcher read the instructions to each class before the participants were allowed to complete them. All participants of both the treatment group and the control group were reassured about the anonymity of their answers. They were also reminded that only the demographic questionnaire had correct answers, that only the researcher would see their answers but would not know who they belonged to, and that their answers would not have any effect on their grades. They were directed to provide correct demographic information and to give their own honest and sincere opinions on the inventories.

Research Question

Is there a relationship between the aesthetic reading of American literature selections from the required curriculum, students' aesthetically-evoked responses to these readings, as presented in their written responses, and students' self-efficacy beliefs relevant to American literature?

Research Hypotheses

First, the null hypothesis is presented, followed by the research or alternative hypothesis. The research or alternative hypothesis designation was recommended by Howell (1989) to avoid confusion between the null and research hypotheses.

Null hypothesis one: There is no relationship or a negative relationship between aesthetically-evoked reader responses and students' self-efficacy beliefs relevant to American literature.

Research or Alternative hypothesis one: There is a positive relationship between aesthetically-evoked reader responses and students' self-efficacy beliefs relevant to American literature.

Null hypothesis two: As measured by the CRAL, the mean posttest level of self-efficacy beliefs regarding American literature for participants who have read selections aesthetically and written aesthetically-evoked reader responses will not differ statistically or will be significantly lower than the mean posttest level of self-efficacy beliefs regarding American literature for participants who do not read selections aesthetically and write aesthetically-evoked reader responses.

Research or Alternative hypothesis two: As measured by the CRAL, the mean posttest level of self-efficacy beliefs regarding American literature for participants who have read selections aesthetically and written aesthetically-evoked reader responses will be significantly higher than the mean posttest level of self-efficacy beliefs regarding American literature for participants who do not read selections aesthetically and write aesthetically-evoked reader responses.

Null hypothesis three: As measured by the CRAL, there is not a significant (sex) x (treatment) interaction between the mean posttest level of self-efficacy beliefs regarding American literature for participants who have read selections aesthetically and written aesthetically-evoked reader responses and the mean posttest level of self-efficacy beliefs regarding American literature for participants who do not read selections aesthetically and write aesthetically-evoked reader responses.

Research or Alternative hypothesis three: As measured by the CRAL, there is a significant (sex) x (treatment) interaction between the mean posttest level of self-efficacy beliefs regarding American literature for participants who have read selections aesthetically and written aesthetically-evoked reader responses and the mean posttest level of self-efficacy beliefs regarding American literature for participants who do not read selections aesthetically and write aesthetically-evoked reader responses.

To test null hypothesis one, a linear regression was performed where the criterion variable, American literature-related self-efficacy, was regressed upon the independent variable, reader response. The researcher first took American literature-related self-efficacy (item level) and regressed it upon total reader response (sum of 10 reader response items; Cronbach's alpha = .90). To gain additional insights into the data, the researcher then regressed item-level American literature-related self-efficacy upon the separate reader response scores from each of the ten classes.

To test null hypothesis two, a 2 (treatment) x 2 (sex) ANCOVA was conducted to measure differences in self-efficacy beliefs regarding comprehension of American literature, the dependent variable, between treatment and control groups, using pretest self-efficacy as a covariate. Sex was included as a variable in his study because prior research (Pajares & Johnson, 1996; Pajares & Miller, 1994, 1995; Tomte & Hatlevik, 2011) had revealed that males and females may have different levels of self-efficacy.

To test null hypothesis three, the interaction resulting from the 2 (sex) x 2 (treatment) ANCOVA was computed.

CHAPTER IV

RESULTS

The purpose of this chapter is to present the results from the intervention of an aesthetic reading and reader response strategy on students' self-efficacy beliefs regarding their comprehension of American literature. The chapter presents sample data, results of analyses of the Confidence in Reading American Literature Survey (CRAL) and statistical tests of the hypotheses.

Sample

All of the participants in this study ($N = 62$), were enrolled in regular English 3/American literature classes in a large Title I high school, which is part of the Miami-Dade County Public School System. See Table 8 for the demographic information of the study participants. The age of the participants ranged from 15 years to 18 years with the average age being 16.56 years. The study sample was comprised of 56% males ($n = 35$) and 44% females ($n = 27$). The sample's racial/ethnic percentages reflected a Hispanic majority and a mixture of other populations: 4.8% were White (non-Hispanic), 35% were Black (non-Hispanic), 56% were Hispanic, and 3.2% were Multiracial. There were no reported Asian/Pacific Islanders or Native Americans in the sample.

Students in a total of four classes ($N = 62$) participated in the study. One teacher taught the two classes that made-up the control group, ($n = 17$) and ($n = 12$) and the researcher taught the two experimental classes, ($n = 17$) and ($n = 16$). See Table 8 for the demographic breakdown of each group. The average age of the participants in the two groups was very similar with 16.59 years in the control group and 16.55 years in the experimental group. Males constituted 59% of the control group and females 41%. Similarly, the experimental group had 55% males and 45% females. Racially/ethnically, both groups were quite close to the school's student population with the control group being comprised of 3.4% White (non-Hispanic), 45% Black (non-Hispanic), and 52% Hispanic; the experimental group was: 6% White, 27% Black (non-Hispanic), 60% Hispanic, and 6% Multiracial.

Table 8

Age, Sex, and Race/Ethnicity Frequency by Control and Experimental Group

Variable	Control Group	Experimental Group	Total
Age			
15	1	1	2
16	13	18	31
17	12	9	21
18	3	5	8
Total	29	33	62
Age M (*SD*)	16.59 (.73)	16.55 (.79)	16.56 (.76)
Sex			
Male	17	18	35
Female	12	15	27
Total	29	33	62
Race/Ethnicity			
White (non-Hispanic)	1	2	3
Black (non-Hispanic)	13	9	22
Hispanic	15	20	35
Asian/Pacific Islander	0	0	0
Native American	0	0	0
Multiracial	0	2	2
Total	29	33	62

Cross Tabulation Analyses of Demographic Variables

The $\chi2$ analyses did not demonstrate statistically significant results for any of the demographic variable combinations (see Table 9). Thus, the researcher can conclude that proportional representation by demographic variable did not differ by group (control or experimental), age (15, 16, 17, or 18), or race/ethnicity, White (non-Hispanic), Black (non-Hispanic), Hispanic, or multi-racial. Consequently, there was evidence that the random assignment was successful in making the two groups equivalent (Fraenkel & Wallen, 2009).

Table 9

Cross Tabulation Results of Demographic Variables

Variable Combination	$\chi2$ value	*df*	*p*
Group and Age	1.48	3	.69
Group and Sex	0.10	1	.75
Group and Race/Ethnicity	3.53	3	.32
Sex and Age	3.75	3	.29
Sex and Race/Ethnicity	2.93	3	.40
Age and Race/Ethnicity	10.28	9	.33

Hypothesis One Results

Null hypothesis one: There is no relationship or a negative relationship between aesthetically-evoked reader responses and students' self-efficacy beliefs relevant to American literature. Linear regressions were employed to test these relationships. In all cases except in the first reader response assignment, where five of the 12 self-efficacy beliefs were positively associated with aesthetically-evoked reader responses, the research hypothesis was not supported (in other words, the null hypothesis was supported). Thus, there was partial support for the first research hypothesis. Specifically, students' American literature self-efficacy beliefs concerning: being able to identify all key points, understanding text, identifying other important references, understanding meaning of each sentence, and recalling important points were positively associated with aesthetically-evoked reader responses in the first response assignment.

The results where 12 linear regressions, (one for each of the CRAL questions), were conducted per reader response assignment (10) are presented below. There was also a linear regression where reader response item score was examined as a total score, followed by the 12 item-level linear regressions. The criterion variable, American literature-related self-efficacy, was regressed upon the independent variable, reader response (the grades on the reader response assignments); the grades for each assignment were coded as numerical values by the researcher: A = 4, B = 3, C = 2, D = 1, and F = 0. Again, the only statistically significant results were found with reader response assignment one (not for total reader response score, however).

Reader Response Assignment #1: *The Call of the Wild* **(London, 1915)**

American literature-related self-efficacy item score regressed on total reader response score:

$r = .07, F(1, 34) = 0.06, r^2 = .002, p = .80$

American literature-related self-efficacy item score regressed on reader response score for assignment #1 only:

Self-Efficacy Question 1: Identify all key points

$r = .41, F(1, 34) = 6.75, r^2 = .166, p = .01$

Self-Efficacy Question 2: Understand text

$r = .36, F(1, 34) = 4.94, r^2 = .127, p = .03$

Self-Efficacy Question 3: Identify other important references

$r = .35, F(1, 34) = 4.67, r^2 = .121, p = .04$

Self-Efficacy Question 4: Answer questions

$r = .18, F(1, 34) = 1.17, r^2 = .033, p = .29$

Self-Efficacy Question 5: Understand meaning of each sentence

$r = .55, F(1, 34) = 14.88, r^2 = .304, p < .001$

Self-Efficacy Question 6: Recall important points

$r = .35, F(1, 34) = 4.84, r^2 = .125, p = .04$

Self-Efficacy Question 7: Understand meaning

$r = .26, F(1, 34) = 2.46, r^2 = .068, p = .13$

Self-Efficacy Question 8: Search for relevant information

$r = .26, F(1, 34) = 2.44, r^2 = .067, p = .13$

Self-Efficacy Question 9: Write notes in own words

$r = .02, F(1, 34) = 0.19, r^2 = .121, p = .89$

Self-Efficacy Question 10: Ask another student if cannot understand

$r = .02, F(1, 34) = 0.00, r^2 = .000, p = .99$

Self-Efficacy Question 11: Use variety of methods

$r = .11$, $F(1, 34) = 0.39$, $r^2 = .011$, $p = .53$

Self-Efficacy Question 12: Select information to write essay

$r = .07$, $F(1, 34) = 0.15$, $r^2 = .004$, $p = .70$

Reader Response Assignment #2: Whitman Poetry
American literature-related self-efficacy item score regressed on total reader response score:

$r = .23$, $F(1, 34) = 1.92$, $r^2 = .05$, $p = .18$

American literature-related self-efficacy item score regressed on reader response score for assignment #2 only:

Self-Efficacy Question 1: Identify all key points

$r = .05$, $F(1, 34) = .101$, $r^2 = .003$, $p = .75$

Self-Efficacy Question 2: Understand text

$r = .094$, $F(1, 34) = .301$, $r^2 = .009$, $p = .59$

Self-Efficacy Question 3: Identify other important references

$r = .05$, $F(1, 34) = .10$, $r^2 = .003$, $p = .76$

Self-Efficacy Question 4: Answer questions

$r = .09$, $F(1, 34) = .264$, $r^2 = .008$, $p = .61$

Self-Efficacy Question 5: Understand meaning of each sentence

$r = .09$, $F(1, 34) = .304$, $r^2 = .009$, $p = .59$

Self-Efficacy Question 6: Recall important points

$r = .04$, $F(1, 34) = .054$, $r^2 = .002$, $p = .82$

Self-Efficacy Question 7: Understand meaning

$r = .04$, $F(1, 34) = .042$, $r^2 = .001$, $p = .84$

Self-Efficacy Question 8: Search for relevant information

$r = .12$, $F(1, 34) = .504$, $r^2 = .015$, $p = .48$

Self-Efficacy Question 9: Write notes in own words

$r = .22$, $F(1, 34) = 1.766$, $r^2 = .049$, $p = .19$

Self-Efficacy Question 10: Ask another student if cannot understand

$r = .004$, $F(1, 34) = 0.00$, $r^2 = .000$, $p = .98$

Self-Efficacy Question 11: Use variety of methods

$r = .31$, $F(1, 34) = 3.605$, $r^2 = .096$, $p = .07$ (marginal significance)

Self-Efficacy Question 12: Select information to write essay

$r = .18$, $F(1, 34) = 1.189$, $r^2 = .034$, $p = .28$

Reader Response Assignment #3: Whitman Poetry
American literature-related self-efficacy item score regressed on total reader response score:

$r = .04$, $F(1, 34) = 0.05$, $r^2 = .002$, $p = .82$

American literature-related self-efficacy item score regressed on reader response score for assignment #3 only:

Self-Efficacy Question 1: Identify all key points

$r = .03$, $F(1, 34) = .026$, $r^2 = .001$, $p = .88$

Self-Efficacy Question 2: Understand text

$r = .02$, $F(1, 34) = .013$, $r^2 = .000$, $p = .92$

Self-Efficacy Question 3: Identify other important references

$r = .19$, $F(1, 34) = 1.306$, $r^2 = .037$, $p = .26$

Self-Efficacy Question 4: Answer questions

$r = .00$, $F(1, 34) = .000$, $r^2 = .000$, $p = .99$

Self-Efficacy Question 5: Understand meaning of each sentence

$r = .02$, $F(1, 34) = .009$, $r^2 = .000$, $p = .93$

Self-Efficacy Question 6: Recall important points

$r = .07, F(1, 34) = .157, r^2 = .005, p = .69$

Self-Efficacy Question 7: Understand meaning

$r = .21, F(1, 34) = 1.504, r^2 = .042, p = .23$

Self-Efficacy Question 8: Search for relevant information

$r = .14, F(1, 34) = .684, r^2 = .020, p = .41$

Self-Efficacy Question 9: Write notes in own words

$r = .01, F(1, 34) = .002, r^2 = .000, p = .97$

Self-Efficacy Question 10: Ask another student if cannot understand

$r = .14, F(1, 34) = .664, r^2 = .019, p = .41$

Self-Efficacy Question 11: Use variety of methods

$r = .01, F(1, 34) = .005, r^2 = .000, p = .94$

Self-Efficacy Question 12: Select information to write essay

$r = .07, F(1, 34) = .183, r^2 = .005, p = .67$

Reader Response Assignment #4: Whitman Poetry
American literature-related self-efficacy item score regressed on total reader response score:

$r = .001, F(1, 34) = 0.00, r2 = .00, p = .99$

American literature-related self-efficacy item score regressed on reader response score for assignment #4 only:

Self-Efficacy Question 1: Identify all key points

$r = .01, F(1, 34) = .002, r^2 = .000, p = .96$

Self-Efficacy Question 2: Understand text

$r = .16, F(1, 34) = .912, r^2 = .026, p = .35$

Self-Efficacy Question 3: Identify other important references

$r = .18, F(1, 34) = 1.070, r^2 = .031, p = .31$

Self-Efficacy Question 4: Answer questions

$r = .01$, $F(1, 34) = .005$, $r^2 = .000$, $p = .94$

Self-Efficacy Question 5: Understand meaning of each sentence

$r = .14$, $F(1, 34) = .717$, $r^2 = .021$, $p = .40$

Self-Efficacy Question 6: Recall important points

$r = .09$, $F(1, 34) = .263$, $r^2 = .008$, $p = .61$

Self-Efficacy Question 7: Understand meaning

$r = .10$, $F(1, 34) = .308$, $r^2 = .009$, $p = .58$

Self-Efficacy Question 8: Search for relevant information

$r = .11$, $F(1, 34) = .440$, $r^2 = .013$, $p = .51$

Self-Efficacy Question 9: Write notes in own words

$r = .17$, $F(1, 34) = .949$, $r^2 = .027$, $p = .34$

Self-Efficacy Question 10: Ask another student if cannot understand

$r = .33$, $F(1, 34) = 4.188$, $r^2 = .110$, $p = .05$ (marginal significance)

Self-Efficacy Question 11: Use variety of methods

$r = .15$, $F(1, 34) = .805$, $r^2 = ..023$, $p = .38$

Self-Efficacy Question 12: Select information to write essay

$r = .18$, $F(1, 34) = 1.115$, $r^2 = .032$, $p = .30$

Reader Response Assignment #5: Dickinson Poetry
American literature-related self-efficacy item score regressed on total reader response score:

$r = .026$, $F(1, 34) = 0.02$, $r^2 = .001$, $p = .88$

American literature-related self-efficacy item score regressed on reader response score for assignment #5 only:

Self-Efficacy Question 1: Identify all key points

$r = .03$, $F(1, 34) = .020$, $r^2 = .001$, $p = .89$

Self-Efficacy Question 2: Understand text

$r = .08$, $F(1, 34) = .192$, $r^2 = .006$, $p = .66$

Self-Efficacy Question 3: Identify other important references

$r = .05$, $F(1, 34) = .083$, $r^2 = .002$, $p = .78$

Self-Efficacy Question 4: Answer questions

$r = .12$, $F(1, 34) = .503$, $r^2 = .015$, $p = .48$

Self-Efficacy Question 5: Understand meaning of each sentence

$r = .12$, $F(1, 34) = .481$, $r^2 = .014$, $p = .49$

Self-Efficacy Question 6: Recall important points

$r = .11$, $F(1, 34) = .378$, $r^2 = .011$, $p = .54$

Self-Efficacy Question 7: Understand meaning

$r = .04$, $F(1, 34) = .041$, $r^2 = .001$, $p = .84$

Self-Efficacy Question 8: Search for relevant information

$r = .25$, $F(1, 34) = .2.168$, $r^2 = .060$, $p = .15$

Self-Efficacy Question 9: Write notes in own words

$r = .09$, $F(1, 34) = .297$, $r^2 = .009$, $p = .59$

Self-Efficacy Question 10: Ask another student if cannot understand

$r = .25$, $F(1, 34) = 2.35$, $r^2 = .065$, $p = .13$

Self-Efficacy Question 11: Use variety of methods

$r = .15$, $F(1, 34) = .821$, $r^2 = .024$, $p = .37$

Self-Efficacy Question 12: Select information to write essay

$r = .22$, $F(1, 34) = 1.752$, $r^2 = .049$, $p = .19$

Reader Response Assignment #6: Dickinson Poetry

American literature-related self-efficacy item score regressed on total reader response score:

$r = .17, F(1, 34) = 0.99, r^2 = .03, p = .33$

American literature-related self-efficacy item score regressed on reader response score for assignment #6 only:

Self-Efficacy Question 1: Identify all key points

$r = .09, F(1, 34) = .274, r^2 = .008, p = .60$

Self-Efficacy Question 2: Understand text

$r = .14, F(1, 34) = .716, r^2 = .021, p = .40$

Self-Efficacy Question 3: Identify other important references

$r = .01, F(1, 34) = .003, r^2 = .000, p = .96$

Self-Efficacy Question 4: Answer questions

$r = .15, F(1, 34) = .758, r^2 = .022, p = .39$

Self-Efficacy Question 5: Understand meaning of each sentence

$r = .04, F(1, 34) = .060, r^2 = .002, p = .81$

Self-Efficacy Question 6: Recall important points

$r = .15, F(1, 34) = .823, r^2 = ..024, p = .37$

Self-Efficacy Question 7: Understand meaning

$r = .01, F(1, 34) = .006, r^2 = .000, p = .94$

Self-Efficacy Question 8: Search for relevant information

$r = .08, F(1, 34) = .226, r^2 = .007, p = .64$

Self-Efficacy Question 9: Write notes in own words

$r = .12, F(1, 34) = .474, r^2 = .014, p = .50$

Self-Efficacy Question 10: Ask another student if cannot understand

$r = .004, F(1, 34) = .001, r^2 = .000, p = .98$

Self-Efficacy Question 11: Use variety of methods

$r = .18, F(1, 34) = 1.153, r^2 = .033, p = .29$

Self-Efficacy Question 12: Select information to write essay

$r = .08, F(1, 34) = .230, r^2 = .007, p = .64$

Reader Response Assignment #7: *Uncle Tom's Cabin* (Stowe, 1899)
American literature-related self-efficacy item score regressed on total reader response score:

$r = .01, F(1, 34) = 0.01, r^2 = .00, p = .94$

American literature-related self-efficacy item score regressed on reader response score for assignment #7 only:

Self-Efficacy Question 1: Identify all key points

$r = .03, F(1, 34) = .030, r^2 = .001, p = .86$

Self-Efficacy Question 2: Understand text

$r = .19, F(1, 34) = 1.233, r^2 = .035, p = .28$

Self-Efficacy Question 3: Identify other important references

$r = .11, F(1, 34) = .402, r^2 = .012, p = .53$

Self-Efficacy Question 4: Answer questions

$r = .04, F(1, 34) = .041, r^2 = .001, p = .84$

Self-Efficacy Question 5: Understand meaning of each sentence

$r = .04, F(1, 34) = .061, r^2 = .002, p = .81$

Self-Efficacy Question 6: Recall important points

$r = .15, F(1, 34) = .779, r^2 = .022, p = .38$

Self-Efficacy Question 7: Understand meaning

$r = .07, F(1, 34) = .175, r^2 = .005, p = .68$

Self-Efficacy Question 8: Search for relevant information

$r = .06$, $F(1, 34) = .106$, $r^2 = .003$, $p = .75$

Self-Efficacy Question 9: Write notes in own words

$r = .08$, $F(1, 34) = .216$, $r^2 = .006$, $p = .65$

Self-Efficacy Question 10: Ask another student if cannot understand

$r = .08$, $F(1, 34) = .244$, $r^2 = .007$, $p = .62$

Self-Efficacy Question 11: Use variety of methods

$r = .08$, $F(1, 34) = .221$, $r^2 = .006$, $p = .64$

Self-Efficacy Question 12: Select information to write essay

$r = .04$, $F(1, 34) = .061$, $r^2 = .002$, $p = .81$

Reader Response Assignment #8: *Uncle Tom's Cabin* (Stowe, 1899)
American literature-related self-efficacy item score regressed on total reader response score:

$r = .00$, $F(1, 34) = 0.00$, $r^2 = .00$, $p = .99$

American literature-related self-efficacy item score regressed on reader response score for assignment #8 only:

Self-Efficacy Question 1: Identify all key points

$r = .20$, $F(1, 34) = 1.439$, $r^2 = .041$, $p = .24$

Self-Efficacy Question 2: Understand text

$r = .01$, $F(1, 34) = .001$, $r^2 = .000$, $p = .97$

Self-Efficacy Question 3: Identify other important references

$r = .003$, $F(1, 34) = .000$, $r^2 = .000$, $p = .98$

Self-Efficacy Question 4: Answer questions

$r = .13$, $F(1, 34) = .605$, $r^2 = .017$, $p = .44$

Self-Efficacy Question 5: Understand meaning of each sentence

$r = .20$, $F(1, 34) = 1.361$, $r^2 = .038$, $p = .25$

Self-Efficacy Question 6: Recall important points

$r = .12$, $F(1, 34) = .528$, $r^2 = .015$, $p = .47$

Self-Efficacy Question 7: Understand meaning

$r = .18$, $F(1, 34) = 1.095$, $r^2 = .031$, $p = .30$

Self-Efficacy Question 8: Search for relevant information

$r = .18$, $F(1, 34) = 1.163$, $r^2 = .033$, $p = .29$

Self-Efficacy Question 9: Write notes in own words

$r = .04$, $F(1, 34) = .065$, $r^2 = .002$, $p = .80$

Self-Efficacy Question 10: Ask another student if cannot understand

$r = .24$, $F(1, 34) = 1.979$, $r^2 = .055$, $p = .17$

Self-Efficacy Question 11: Use variety of methods

$r = .04$, $F(1, 34) = .056$, $r^2 = .002$, $p = .82$

Self-Efficacy Question 12: Select information to write essay

$r = .23$, $F(1, 34) = 1.876$, $r^2 = .052$, $p = .18$

Reader Response Assignment #9: *Uncle Tom's Cabin* (Stowe, 1899)
American literature-related self-efficacy item score regressed on total reader response score:

$r = .04$, $F(1, 34) = 0.05$, $r^2 = .00$, $p = .83$

American literature-related self-efficacy item score regressed on reader response score for assignment #9 only:

Self-Efficacy Question 1: Identify all key points

$r = .07$, $F(1, 34) = .186$, $r^2 = .005$, $p = .67$

Self-Efficacy Question 2: Understand text

$r = .05$, $F(1, 34) = .088$, $r^2 = .003$, $p = .77$

Self-Efficacy Question 3: Identify other important references

$r = .06, F(1, 34) = .131, r^2 = .004, p = .72$

Self-Efficacy Question 4: Answer questions

$r = .05, F(1, 34) = .088, r^2 = .004, p = .74$

Self-Efficacy Question 5: Understand meaning of each sentence

$r = .05, F(1, 34) = .074, r^2 = .002, p = .79$

Self-Efficacy Question 6: Recall important points

$r = .20, F(1, 34) = 1.359, r^2 = .038, p = .25$

Self-Efficacy Question 7: Understand meaning

$r = .08, F(1, 34) = .219, r^2 = .006, p = .64$

Self-Efficacy Question 8: Search for relevant information

$r = .15, F(1, 34) = .808, r^2 = .023, p = .38$

Self-Efficacy Question 9: Write notes in own words

$r = .14, F(1, 34) = .645, r^2 = .019, p = .43$

Self-Efficacy Question 10: Ask another student if cannot understand

$r = .08, F(1, 34) = .193, r^2 = .006, p = .66$

Self-Efficacy Question 11: Use variety of methods

$r = .01, F(1, 34) = 002, r^2 = .000, p = .97$

Self-Efficacy Question 12: Select information to write essay

$r = .10, F(1, 34) = .352, r^2 = .010, p = .56$

Reader Response Assignment #10: *Uncle Tom's Cabin* (Stowe, 1899)
American literature-related self-efficacy item score regressed on total reader response score:

$r = .11, F(1, 34) = 0.40, r^2 = .01, p = .53$

American literature-related self-efficacy item score regressed on reader response score for assignment #10 only:

Self-Efficacy Question 1: Identify all key points

$r = .02$, $F(1, 34) = .011$, $r^2 = .000$, $p = .92$

Self-Efficacy Question 2: Understand text

$r = .32$, $F(1, 34) = 3.779$, $r^2 = .100$, $p = .06$ (marginal significance)

Self-Efficacy Question 3: Identify other important references

$r = .03$, $F(1, 34) = .022$, $r^2 = .001$, $p = .88$

Self-Efficacy Question 4: Answer questions

$r = .01$, $F(1, 34) = .004$, $r^2 = .000$, $p = .95$

Self-Efficacy Question 5: Understand meaning of each sentence

$r = .05$, $F(1, 34) = .097$, $r^2 = .003$, $p = .76$

Self-Efficacy Question 6: Recall important points

$r = .12$, $F(1, 34) = .516$, $r^2 = .015$, $p = .48$

Self-Efficacy Question 7: Understand meaning

$r = .06$, $F(1, 34) = .131$, $r^2 = .004$, $p = .72$

Self-Efficacy Question 8: Search for relevant information

$r = .16$, $F(1, 34) = .868$, $r^2 = .025$, $p = .36$

Self-Efficacy Question 9: Write notes in own words

$r = .14$, $F(1, 34) = .643$, $r^2 = .019$, $p = .43$

Self-Efficacy Question 10: Ask another student if cannot understand

$r = .11$, $F(1, 34) = .399$, $r^2 = .012$, $p = .53$

Self-Efficacy Question 11: Use variety of methods

$r = .01$, $F(1, 34) = .002$, $r^2 = .000$, $p = .96$

Self-Efficacy Question 12: Select information to write essay

$r = .17$, $F(1, 34) = .948$, $r^2 = .027$, $p = .34$

Hypothesis Two Results

Null hypothesis two: As measured by the CRAL, the mean posttest level of self-efficacy beliefs regarding American literature for participants who have read selections aesthetically and written aesthetically-evoked reader responses will not differ statistically or will be significantly lower than the mean posttest level of self-efficacy beliefs regarding American literature for participants who do not read selections aesthetically and write aesthetically-evoked reader responses.

To test null hypothesis two, a series of 2 (treatment) x 2 (sex) ANCOVAs were conducted to measure differences in self-efficacy beliefs regarding comprehension of American literature between treatment and control groups, using pretest self-efficacy as a covariate. Pre- and post- measures of each of the 12 separate self-efficacy items were used in the analyses; thus, there were 12 separate ANCOVA analyses to test the hypothesis.

A series of preliminary analyses were conducted to evaluate the homogeneity of slopes assumption using American literature self-efficacy posttest scores as a dependent variable, American literature self-efficacy pretest scores as a covariate, and group (treatment, control) and sex (male, female) as the independent variables. The findings suggested that the relationship between the covariate and the dependent variable in each of the 12 analyses did not differ significantly as a function of the independent variables $Fs(1, 57) = 0.01 - 2.81$, $ps > .05$. In addition, for each of the 12 ANCOVAs, the Levene's test results revealed equal variances among groups, $Fs(3, 58) = 0.02 - 2.68$, $ps > .05$; thus, homogeneity of variance was assumed. There was not a significant main sex effect for any of the analyses, but there was a significant main effect for treatment group in seven of the 12 ANCOVAs. In addition, in all cases, the statistically significant effect sizes were relatively modest; yet, they fell within the range of the aforementioned research studies, even though those studies dealt with participants of different ages, different types of reading comprehension strategies, and ran for different time periods than this study (e.g., Bandura & Schunk, 1981; McCabe et al., 2006; McCrudden et al., 2005; Naseri, 2012; Nelson & Manset-Williamson, 2006; and Van Keer & Verhaeghe, 2005).

Self-Efficacy Item 1: Identify all key points

After adjustment for the self-efficacy pre-test score (item 1), the ANCOVA was not significant for treatment group $F(1, 57) = .01$, $p = .93$, $\eta2 = .00$ or sex $F(1, 57) = 1.51$, $p = .22$, $\eta2 = .03$. The interaction between treatment group and sex was not significant as well $F(1, 57) = .42$, $p = .52$, $\eta2 = .01$. Thus, treatment group self-efficacy as it related to identifying all key points did not significantly improve as compared to the control group. Neither sex nor the treatment group x sex interaction was significant as well. Therefore, the null hypothesis was supported.

Self-Efficacy Item 2: Understand text

After adjustment for the self-efficacy pre-test score (item 2), the ANCOVA was not significant for treatment group $F(1, 57) = .04$, $p = .85$, $\eta 2 = .00$ or sex $F(1, 57) = .01$, $p = .93$, $\eta 2 = .00$. The interaction between treatment group and sex was not significant $F(1, 57) = .01$, $p = .91$, $\eta 2 = .00$. Thus, treatment group self-efficacy as it related to understanding text did not significantly improve as compared to the control group. Sex and the treatment group x sex interaction were not significant. Consequently, the null hypothesis was supported.

Self-Efficacy Item 3: Identify other important references

After adjustment for the self-efficacy pre-test score (item 3), the ANCOVA was not significant for treatment group $F(1, 57) = 1.26$, $p = .27$, $\eta 2 = .02$ or sex $F(1, 57) = .01$, $p = .94$, $\eta 2 = .00$. The interaction between treatment group and sex was not significant $F(1, 57) = 1.09$, $p = .30$, $\eta 2 = .02$. Therefore, treatment group self-efficacy as it related to identifying other important references did not significantly improve as compared to the control group. Sex and the treatment group x sex interaction were not significant. Thus, the null hypothesis was supported.

Self-Efficacy Item 4: Answer questions

After adjustment for the self-efficacy pre-test score (item 4), the ANCOVA was significant for treatment group $F(1, 57) = 4.01$, $p = .04$, $\eta 2 = .07$, but not for sex $F(1, 57) = 3.00$, $p = .09$, $\eta 2 = .05$. The interaction between treatment group and sex was not significant $F(1, 57) = .99$, $p = .32$, $\eta 2 = .02$. Thus, treatment group self-efficacy as it related answering questions significantly improved as compared to the control group. Neither sex nor the treatment group x sex interaction was significant. Because the treatment group's posttest self-efficacy adjusted group mean was significantly higher than the control group's adjusted group mean, the research hypothesis was supported.

Self-Efficacy Item 5: Understand meaning of each sentence

After adjustment for the self-efficacy pre-test score (item 5), the ANCOVA was not significant for treatment group $F(1, 57) = .28$, $p = .60$, $\eta 2 = .01$ or sex $F(1, 57) = .88$, $p = .35$, $\eta 2 = .02$. The interaction between treatment group and sex was not significant $F(1, 57) = .69$, $p = .41$, $\eta 2 = .01$. Therefore, treatment group self-efficacy as it related to understanding the meaning of each sentence did not significantly improve as compared to the control group. Neither sex nor the treatment group x sex interaction was significant. Consequently, the null hypothesis was supported.

Self-Efficacy Item 6: Recall important points

After adjustment for the self-efficacy pre-test score (item 6), the ANCOVA was not significant for treatment group $F(1, 57) = 2.48$, $p = .12$, $\eta2 = .04$ or sex $F(1, 57) = 2.35$, $p = .13$, $\eta2 = .04$. The interaction between treatment group and sex was not significant $F(1, 57) = .09$, $p = .76$, $\eta2 = .00$. Thus, treatment group self-efficacy as it related to recalling important points did not significantly improve as compared to the control group. Neither sex nor the treatment group x sex interaction was significant as well. Therefore, the null hypothesis was supported.

Self-Efficacy Item 7: Understand meaning

After adjustment for the self-efficacy pre-test score (item 7), the ANCOVA was significant for treatment group $F(1, 57) = 4.66$, $p = .04$, $\eta2 = .08$, but not for sex $F(1, 57) = 1.14$, $p = .29$, $\eta2 = .02$. The interaction between treatment group and sex was not significant $F(1, 57) = .01$, $p = .91$, $\eta2 = .00$. Thus, treatment group self-efficacy as it related to understanding meaning significantly improved as compared to the control group. Neither sex nor the treatment group x sex interaction was significant. Because the treatment group's posttest self-efficacy adjusted group mean was significantly higher than the control group's adjusted group mean, the research hypothesis was supported.

Self-Efficacy Item 8: Search for relevant information

After adjustment for the self-efficacy pre-test score (item 8), the ANCOVA was significant for treatment group $F(1, 57) = 4.05$, $p = .049$, $\eta2 = .07$, but not for sex $F(1, 57) = 2.17$, $p = .15$, $\eta2 = .04$. The interaction between treatment group and sex was not significant as well $F(1, 57) = .16$, $p = .69$, $\eta2 = .00$. Thus, treatment group self-efficacy as it related to searching for relevant information significantly improved as compared to the control group. However, neither sex nor the treatment group x sex interaction was significant. As the treatment group's posttest self-efficacy adjusted group mean was significantly higher than the control group's adjusted group mean, the research hypothesis was supported.

Self-Efficacy Item 9: Write notes in own words

After adjustment for the self-efficacy pre-test score (item 9), the ANCOVA was significant for treatment group $F(1, 57) = 4.15$, $p = .04$, $\eta2 = .07$, but not for sex $F(1, 57) = .31$, $p = .56$, $\eta2 = .01$. The interaction between treatment group and sex was not significant $F(1, 57) = .01$, $p = .95$, $\eta2 = .00$. Thus, treatment group self-efficacy as it related to writing notes in own words significantly improved as compared to the control group. Neither sex nor the treatment group x sex interaction was significant. For the reason that the treatment group's posttest self-efficacy adjusted group mean was significantly higher than the control group's adjusted group mean, the research hypothesis was supported.

Self-Efficacy Item 10: Understand text if ask student for assistance

After adjustment for the self-efficacy pre-test score (item 10), the ANCOVA was significant for treatment group $F(1, 57) = 4.03$, $p = .04$, $\eta2 = .07$, but not for sex $F(1, 57) = .01$, $p = .98$, $\eta2 = .00$. The interaction between treatment group and sex was not significant $F(1, 57) = .02$, $p = .90$, $\eta2 = .00$. Thus, treatment group self-efficacy as it related to being able to understand text after asking student for assistance significantly improved as compared to the control group. However, neither sex nor the treatment group x sex interaction was significant. Because the treatment group's posttest self-efficacy adjusted group mean was significantly higher than the control group's adjusted group mean, the research hypothesis was supported.

Self-Efficacy Item 11: Use variety of methods to aid understanding

After adjustment for the self-efficacy pre-test score (item 11), the ANCOVA was significant for treatment group $F(1, 57) = 4.11$, $p = .04$, $\eta2 = .07$, but not for sex $F(1, 57) = .95$, $p = .33$, $\eta2 = .02$. The interaction between treatment group and sex was not significant as well $F(1, 57) = .03$, $p = .86$, $\eta2 = .00$. Thus, treatment group self-efficacy as it related to being able to use a variety of methods to aid understanding significantly improved as compared to the control group. Neither sex nor the treatment group x sex interaction was significant. As the treatment group's posttest self-efficacy adjusted group mean was significantly higher than the control group's adjusted group mean, the research hypothesis was supported.

Self-Efficacy Item 12: Select appropriate information from text to write essay

After adjustment for the self-efficacy pre-test score (item 12), the ANCOVA was significant for treatment group $F(1, 57) = 4.78$, $p = .03$, $\eta2 = .08$, but not for sex $F(1, 57) = .02$, $p = .88$, $\eta2 = .00$. The interaction between treatment group and sex was not significant as well $F(1, 57) = 2.57$, $p = .11$, $\eta2 = .04$. Thus, treatment group self-efficacy as it related to being able to select appropriate information from text to write an essay significantly improved as compared to the control group. However, neither sex nor the treatment group x sex interaction was significant. Inasmuch as the treatment group's posttest self-efficacy adjusted group mean was significantly higher than the control group's adjusted group mean, the research hypothesis was supported.

Hypothesis Three Results

Null hypothesis three: As measured by the CRAL, there is not a significant (sex) x (treatment) interaction between the mean posttest level of self-efficacy beliefs regarding American literature for participants who have read selections aesthetically and written aesthetically-evoked reader responses and the mean posttest level of self-efficacy beliefs regarding American literature for participants who do not read selections aesthetically and write aesthetically-evoked reader responses.

To test null hypothesis three, the interaction resulting from the 2 (sex) x 2 (treatment) ANCOVA was computed. As presented above in each of the ANCOVA analyses by self-efficacy item, there was not a statistically significant interaction; therefore, the null hypothesis was supported for each of the 12 analyses.

Summary

This chapter has presented the results of this quasi-experimental research where there was partial support for research hypotheses one and two: (a) aesthetically-evoked reader responses were related to self-efficacy in American literature and (b) the treatment group's self-efficacy in American literature scores improved significantly over the control group. Null hypothesis three was supported as there was no interaction resulting from the 2 (sex) x 2 (treatment) ANCOVA in each of the 12 analyses. Chapter 5 will present a brief summary of the findings and discuss its implications for research and practice.

CHAPTER V

DISCUSSION

The purpose of this chapter is to discuss the results of this study. It examined the effects on students' self-efficacy beliefs regarding their comprehension of American literature after a two-part intervention of aesthetic reading and reader response strategy was implemented. A brief study summary begins the chapter, which is followed by a discussion of the research hypotheses and analyses. The rest of the chapter discusses the implications of the results of this study for practice and for future research and the limitations of the study conclude the chapter.

Summary of the Study

This study used a quasi-experimental pretest-posttest design to measure the effects of the two-step strategy of aesthetic reading and reader response, implemented as one intervention, on students' self-efficacy beliefs regarding their comprehension of American literature. This study took place in a large Title 1 magnet high school in South Florida where the majority of the participants were Hispanic. The study participants were enrolled in four, regular-level, 11th grade/ English 3/American literature classrooms. One teacher and the researcher were involved in the study with each having two classes. The teacher was assigned to the two control classes that were determined by coin flips conducted by the English Department Head, (who was not involved in the study), from the convenience sample of six classes available to the study. The researcher was assigned to the two treatment classes that were also determined by coin flips conducted by the same person, from the convenience sample of six available classes. All four classes took the modified Confidence in Reading American Literature (CRAL) Survey for the pretest and posttest. As recommended by Bandura (1997), this survey was modified to specifically measure a student's perceived self-efficacy beliefs regarding the various tasks revolving around his/her comprehension of American literature.

The researcher's measure satisfied both Bandura's (1977, 2006) and Pajares' (1997) requirements for an appropriate domain-specific perceived self-efficacy scale. The CRAL Survey used in this research was a modified Self Efficacy Belief in Reading scale (SER: see Appendix E) that was created by Prat-Sala & Redford (2010). The CRAL, like the original, is a 12-item survey. However, it uses a 4-point Likert scale in place of the original scale's 7-point Likert scale. Before the study began, a comparable, regular English 3 class of 25 students took the CRAL survey. This class was in the same school, but it was not involved in the study. This pilot survey had several purposes: establish the administration time of the survey, test the clarity of the survey's instructions, determine if any of the students had difficulty understanding any of the questions, and ascertain if the response choices, the 4-point Likert scale, posed any problems. The study took place over the time period of eight classes. The school followed a block schedule and each student was enrolled in eight classes. The odd classes (periods 1, 3, 5, & 7), alternated days with the even classes (periods 2, 4, 6, and 8). Because of this configuration, the time period of the study was three weeks.

Both the control group and the treatment group read the literature selections designated by the school district for those particular weeks in the grading period. At the beginning of the study period, the researcher explained and modeled aesthetic reading with the treatment group; reader response writing was also modeled by the researcher and practiced by the students. The control group received the regular instruction as indicated by the school district during the study period (MDCPS, 2012). Over the course of the eight classes, the literature text selections were the same for both groups and included: poems by Walt Whitman, poems by Emily Dickinson, and several chapters of Harriet Beecher Stowe's, *Uncle Tom's Cabin,* (1899). The one exception was the literature used by the treatment group for practicing aesthetic reading and writing aesthetically-evoked reader responses. The literature used for these sessions was several excerpts from Jack London's *The Call of the Wild* (1915).

A total of ten reader response assignments had been assigned to the treatment group during the course of the study. One of the ten reader assignments was part of the aesthetic reading/reader response writing practice sessions which took place on the first two days of the study and occurred with the treatment group only. The control group's assignments were the regular assignments that were delineated in the District's pacing guide (MDCPS, 2012).

Discussion of Research Hypotheses

Research Hypothesis One

Research hypothesis 1 stated that there is a positive relationship between aesthetically-evoked reader responses and students' American literature self-efficacy beliefs. The results partially supported this hypothesis as self-efficacy beliefs regarding American literature were found via the linear regression analyses to be related to aesthetically-evoked reader responses in the first session.

Research Hypothesis Two

Research hypothesis 2 stated that: the mean posttest level of self-efficacy beliefs regarding American literature for participants who have read selections aesthetically and written aesthetically-evoked reader responses will be significantly higher than the mean posttest level of self-efficacy beliefs regarding American literature for participants who do not read selections aesthetically and write aesthetically-evoked reader responses. The results partially supported this hypothesis as significant posttest differences in self-efficacy beliefs relevant to the comprehension of American literature were found between the two groups, with the experimental group demonstrating significantly higher posttest self-efficacy scores on seven of the 12 scales.

Research Hypothesis Three

Research hypothesis three stated that: As measured by the CRAL, there is a significant (sex) x (treatment) interaction between the mean posttest level of self-efficacy beliefs regarding American literature for participants who have read selections aesthetically and written aesthetically-evoked reader responses and the mean posttest level of self-efficacy beliefs regarding American literature for participants who do not read selections aesthetically and write aesthetically-evoked reader responses. The results did not support this hypothesis because the computed interaction resulting from the 2 (sex) x 2 (treatment) ANCOVA did not demonstrate a significant interaction; therefore, the research hypothesis was not supported.

Interpretations and Related Implications

The innovative features of this study made it unique in a number of ways. No prior studies were found that had addressed the effects of the two-part intervention of aesthetic reading of literature selections and writing aesthetically-evoked reader responses on students' self-efficacy beliefs. Additionally, no other studies had engaged this treatment regarding the self-efficacy beliefs of high school students, or the effects of this treatment on high school students' self-efficacy beliefs relevant to English 3/American literature class. The American literature course is required throughout the United States as a requirement for graduation; this increases the importance of the study's results.

Several aspects of the study were necessary for compliance with the school district's mandates. The literature selections for both the control group and the treatment group were in accordance with the requisite selections for those weeks in the grading period, as specified by the instructional pacing guide (MDCPS, 2012). The other aspect was that the students in the treatment group received official grades on their written reader response assignments. This aspect had been explained to all the study class students when the classes were selected from the convenience sample for study participation and before the treatment group classes and control group classes had been randomly determined; consent and assent forms had not been delivered to the students. These grades fulfilled the grade requirements for the three-week time period. However, to lessen the chance that the study participants' overall grade average for the nine week grading period would affect the self-efficacy posttest results, the posting of the reader response assignment grades did not occur until after the study's posttests were completed.

One part of the compliance to the district's mandates related to the literature selections used in the study. Although the literature texts were the same, the actual classroom instruction differed greatly between the control group and the treatment group. The instruction in the control group, as required by the district, was consistent with Applebee's (1993) research which had been based on a number of large scale surveys and classroom observations, " Neither...[surveys or observations]...revealed much teaching that reflects truly student-centered philosophies of teaching and learning" (p. 253). The district's focus, which conformed to the state's focus, concentrated on the preparation for standardized tests which included: efferent reading for test-like information, learning literary terms, learning the text vocabulary, discussing the standardized author's meaning, and discussing the traditionally-accepted relationship between the author's meaning and the historical times. All of the academic interactions and activities centered on these concepts. In essence, the district's requirements brought the students' attention to the generally-accepted meanings of the literature, which, according to Rosenblatt (1995), prevented the activation or assimilation of personal ideas or feelings towards or about the text selections that were read. The classroom instruction for the control group during the study period was specified by the district, and the overall, clear purpose was to attempt to help students achieve higher scores on standardized tests (MDCPS, 2012). This instruction exemplified the input/output ideology (Edelsky, 1991; Powell 2009) that is routinely promoted as a result of the high-stakes testing movement.

The instruction in the treatment group during the eight classes of the study demonstrated a contrast to the control group instruction. The class read the texts aesthetically; at times, the students wanted to take turns reading the text aloud, and at other times they elected to read silently. They were encouraged to jot things down during this reading for later comment or question. Any discussions that evolved were based on the students' reactions and connections to what they were reading. The students were made aware of the literary terms, but there was no specific instruction about them. If a student asked for more information, he/she was directed to the textbook and classroom dictionaries, and he/she was told to ask for more help at any time. There were no formal discussions, rather, as the students' engaged with the text individually (after a silent second reading if they chose), they were free to raise their hands so that the researcher could walk over and assist them.

The researcher's assistance during the classes was usually in the form of assuring students that their individual responses were acceptable. The basis for the necessity of this researcher to student support became obvious to both the treatment group researcher and the control group teacher (who had observed the classes), after it had happened a few times. Looking for the *right answer or the answer that the teacher wanted* (efferent reading), was such a habit with these high school students that they had to be given support and reassurance quite often during the first few assignments; many of them were astounded that their personal transactions with the texts, their aesthetically-evoked responses, were acceptable.

The treatment group's post-reading reader response activities were 100% student-based, authentic use of print activities (Langer, 1994, 1998). The instruction flowed as the students developed their understandings of the texts. Students' responses developed in length, description, and complexity as the study time progressed, but each student's progress was unique. The individualized nature of the aesthetically-evoked reader responses provided the medium for each student's expression as he/she transacted with the text (Karolides, 1992; Rosenblatt, 1938, 1978, 1993, 1995, 2003; Willinsky, 1990). For the most part, each student's reader responses to the text quotes that they chose became gradually richer with personalized transactions as the study progressed. They were usually interesting to read because they provided unique insights into the individuals that wrote them. These insights included things like the students': childhoods, families, extended families, cultures, accidents, experiences, religious beliefs, memories, fears, and hopes. This experience leaves the researcher wondering how rich these transactions could become should this type of response be a regular part of the English 3/American literature curriculum.

Because the reading of literature from earlier time periods can be a complicated task, high school students sometimes will require more time to complete and comprehend it. American literature in the English 3 classes exemplifies this issue because it is taught historically in the State of Florida and is purportedly in alignment with the students' American history class (FLDOE, 1997; MDCPS 2012). The study started during the fifth week of the school year and ended during the eighth week, which placed its inception halfway through the first nine week grading period of the school year. The literature selections for this time were from early American texts. This literature was very different from most of the literature that students have had to cope with in their English classes up to that point. The difficulty of the subject matter for adolescents is one of the central reasons that both American history and American literature are taught when the students are in their junior year of high school, rather than in their freshman or sophomore year.

High school students often find early American literature to be difficult and frustrating; based on students' comments there are several reasons for this. The language of the literature is much more formal than the literature that they are used to reading, and it requires a certain level of maturity and reading comprehension skill for students to be able to study the text selections. Moreover, the literature deals with a totally different society than 21st century America, with vastly different morals, ethics, religious beliefs, prejudices, and politics. Ideally, studying the history of America simultaneously with studying about the literature of the same time period is a logical construct. However, it is only hypothetically sound as the reality is full of complexities. There was no evidence of planning between the English department and the Social Studies department at the site school, which resulted in the teachers rarely, if ever, coordinating their instruction about the same historical period. Instead of having knowledge about the time period of the literature, many of the students demonstrated confusion during the study period when they were asked questions about the historical occurrences. All of these factors about the literature may have been more significant to the results of the study than the researcher could have predicted.

Additionally, no studies could be found that involved the effects on students' self-efficacy beliefs relevant to American literature when an aesthetic reading and aesthetically-evoked reader response intervention was implemented. The types of assignments that were used in the studies that were available, (Bandura & Schunk, 1981; 2005; McCabe et al., 2006; McCrudden et al., 2005; Naseri, 2012; Nelson & Manset-Williamson; Van Keer & Verhaeghe, 2005) involved the effects on students' self-efficacy beliefs using other types of reading strategies as students engaged with other types of texts. Logically then, it is possible that the intervention, which required the students to read and comprehend the American literature texts, may have required more time. At best, the study's time period could only be approximated. Based on the reader response results, although admittedly preliminary, the teacher and researcher involved in the study professionally believe that the richness of the reader responses might have continued to increase had the study time been longer.

Research Hypothesis One

Various factors may have influenced the results of Research hypothesis one. The results partially supported a positive relationship between aesthetically-evoked reader responses and students' self-efficacy beliefs relevant to American literature. Despite the researcher being guided by prior research as to the time length, one of the factors may be that the time allotted for the study may not have been adequate to greatly increase the self-efficacy beliefs of the treatment group across the complex domain of American literature comprehension, which is comprised of numerous skills. As previously discussed, the students may have been so deeply indoctrinated in efferent-based instruction that it took them awhile to adjust to the freedom of expression that they were allowed with the aesthetically-evoked reader response assignments.

In addition, quite a few studies (Hackett & Betz, 1989; Pajares, 1996; Pajares & Miller, 1994) have revealed that, " Indeed, most students are over-confident about their academic abilities" (Pajares, 1997, p. 19), and people's accuracy of self-efficacy beliefs, '...cannot easily be divorced from issues of well-being, optimism, and will' (Bandura, 1997, as cited in Pajares, 1997). Therefore, these two factors could have influenced the results of Research hypothesis one. One the one hand, the positive relationship between aesthetically-evoked reader responses and students' self-efficacy beliefs relevant to American literature may have been significantly stronger if the study had been considerably longer. On the other hand, the study participants may have inaccurately reported, or over-estimated, their self-efficacy beliefs regarding their comprehension of American literature on the CRAL. A combination of these two factors could have had considerable effects on the results of Research hypothesis one.

Another element that may have dampened the magnitude of relationship between aesthetically-evoked reader responses and students' self-efficacy beliefs relevant to American literature (Research hypothesis one), was brought to light by Hamill's (2003) research. Her study offered some insights into the self-efficacy beliefs of adolescents that may be applicable to the present study. It involved 43, 16-19 year old high school students who participated in measurements of their "... self-efficacy, perceptions of control, response to stress, persistence and coping mechanisms" (p. 115). The measurements identified four separate groups, but information about two of the groups may be relevant. One group was labeled the "resilient" adolescents, those who had developed "...competence in the face of adversity" (p. 115), "...or more specifically, [resiliency] refers to a dynamic process of positive adaptation and development while simultaneously facing a significant amount of adversity (Luthar, Cicchetti & Becker, 2000, as cited in Hamill 2003, p.115). The other group was labeled the "competent" adolescents, those who had scored "...higher than one-half a standard deviation above the sample mean on all of the...competence measures" (p. 122). Her findings indicated that these two groups measured very similarly in all of the constructs, including self-efficacy beliefs, and supported the study's hypothesis that "...self-efficacy is a trait present among competent adolescents facing adversity (Hamill, 2003, p. 124).

Being cautious about generalizing from her results, Hamill's (2003) findings about resilient adolescents may be pertinent to this study's results for several reasons. It is plausible that most of the intervention's participants were, or had been, facing some type of adversity. This notion is supported by the following information: (a)

36% of the treatment group had already retaken the state's standardized 10th grade reading comprehension test (FCAT), and therefore were behind in school; (b) 22% of the treatment group had already retaken the FCAT more than once; and were therefore one year or more behind in school; (c) 81% of the treatment group had to retake the test again in October, 2013; this meant that being juniors at the time of the study, they were very definitely in danger of not graduating on time and/or receiving a certificate of completion instead of a standard diploma; and (d) 79% of the school's population was receiving free or reduced lunch (FLDOE, 2013a), which meant that 79% of the students' household incomes were low enough to meet the federal guidelines for food assistance for children. As defined by Hamill (2003) and Luthar et al. (2000), most of the participants in this study's treatment population were facing adversity. Thus, they would be considered to be resilient adolescents in Hamill's terms.

Further, Hamill's (2003) study found that these resilient adolescents had similar self-efficacy beliefs when compared to competent adolescents. "Those who are self-efficacious are also more likely to reject negative thoughts about themselves or their abilities than those with a sense of personal inefficacy" (Ozer & Bandura, 1990, as cited in Hamill, 2003, p. 116). Again, being careful about generalizing, the treatment group might have self-reported unrealistically high levels of self-efficacy beliefs on the pretest, or on both the pretest and the posttest (Pajares, 1997; Sanders-Reio, 2010).

Research Hypothesis Two

Research hypothesis two was partially supported by the study's results. The treatment group's mean posttest level of self-efficacy beliefs regarding American literature was significantly higher than the control group's mean posttest level of self-efficacy beliefs regarding the comprehension of American literature on a majority of scales. Pre- and post- measures of each of the 12 separate self-efficacy items on the modified CRAL were used in the analyses, which resulted in 12 separate ANCOVA analyses to test the hypothesis.

Seven of the twelve analyses supported the research hypothesis. These results returned the researcher to review the analyses of the questions that had confirmed that varying levels of functioning were evident. The analysis review, based on Bloom's Taxonomy (1956) of the thinking/learning levels of the questions, revealed information useful to this discussion. Next, each CRAL survey question that supported Research hypothesis two is described using Bloom's Taxonomy (1956) as the criterion:

Question #4 - After you have read a text, how well can you answer questions on it? When analyzed, this question incorporates all levels of thinking/learning:

knowledge, comprehension, application, analysis, synthesis and evaluation. This is because the designated textbook for this class, (and the ninth and 10th grades textbooks as well), incorporates all the levels of questioning in each post-reading section. When asked about answering questions after reading a text, it was possible that the textbook questions, the students' most-likely frame of reference for English 3 class, were the bases for their reasoning when they answered this question.

Question #7 – Before you answer a question about the text, how well have you understood the meaning of the question? When analyzed, this question requires the student to utilize the middle levels of thinking/learning which are comprehension and application. Understanding the question and then being able to answer the question, which is application, seems to be implied in this question.

Question #8 – How well can you search effectively for relevant information in a text from your American literature book when you are asked to find support for an answer you have given? This question requires thinking/learning levels at the middle range –comprehension and application, because one has to be able to understand the question and then apply this understanding by finding an answer. However, the three highest levels- analysis, synthesis and evaluation are also involved here. One must analyze the text for adequate and logical support, draw the information together, and then evaluate the information you have found and pulled together; the next step would be to see if this information is relevant and provides adequate support for the answer you have already provided.

Question #9 – When reading in your American literature book, how well can you write notes in your own words? This question involves the three highest levels of thinking/learning - analysis, synthesis and evaluation. The respondent would analyze what needed to be notated, pull the information together, and then determine if these notes were appropriate for his/her needs.

Question #10 – If you cannot understand a text in your American literature book, how well can you understand it if you ask another student in you class about it? This question involves the three highest levels of thinking/learning – analysis, synthesis and evaluation. The respondent would have to analyze exactly what is perplexing him/her, pull this together into some sort of logical question, ask another student the question, and then evaluate their understanding (again).

Question #11 – How well can you use a variety of different methods to enable your understanding of a text in your American literature book? (e.g., writing notes, printing pages from the online book and highlighting or underlining, etc.?) This question incorporates all the levels of thinking/learning: knowledge, comprehension, application, analysis, synthesis and evaluation. The respondent would have to have the knowledge of doing the other methods, understand what they know and do not know from the text, apply that information to determine what other methods are necessary, analyze the text, pull it all together and use the other methods chosen, and then evaluate what they have done.

Question #12 – How well can you select the most appropriate information from a text in you American literature book when you are asked to write an essay? This question incorporates all the levels of thinking/learning: knowledge, comprehension, application, analysis, synthesis and evaluation. Although other questions required the respondent to use of all six levels of thinking/learning, this particular question is probably the one of highest difficulty. This is based on the notion that creating an essay is a requirement that relies on all the levels of thinking/learning, but the essay itself is a separate and new production that is also regarded as a formal academic assignment that is usually assessed as such by ELAR teachers.

The analyses of these questions revealed that the increase in self-efficacy beliefs regarding American literature occurred predominantly in areas that required three or more levels of thinking, (question #7 was the exception). Bloom's Taxonomy (1956) is a generally-accepted theory of learning domains, and the six categories of thinking/learning are considered as degrees of functioning difficulties (Luebke & Lorie, 2013; McBain, 2011; Pogrow, 1993; Seaman, 2011). Inherent in this belief is the construct that the first level of thinking must be mastered before the next level may take place and so on through the six levels, although there is argument in the educational community about how this construct actually works, which has led to some revisions in the taxonomy that are still being disputed (Seaman, 2011).

An application of this construct to the seven questions that showed significant increases in self-efficacy beliefs revealed that three of these questions required all the levels of thinking/learning: knowledge, comprehension, application, analysis, synthesis and evaluation. Two of the seven questions involved the three highest levels of thinking, analysis, synthesis, and evaluation, which can be taken to mean that the students, having already mastered the three lower levels, or were not really cognizant of using them as resources to answer the question (McBain, 2011; Seaman, 2011). One of the seven questions necessitated the use of the two middle levels of thinking/learning, comprehension and application, but also required the three highest levels of thinking, analysis, synthesis, and evaluation; again, this could mean that the first level of thinking/learning had already been mastered, or that students were not aware of using this resource. The remaining one question involved the two middle levels of thinking, comprehension and application, which indicated that the first level, knowledge, had been grasped; possibly, students were not aware of using the first level as a resource (McBain, 2011; Seaman, 2011).

Subsequent analyses of the questions that did not show significant increases in self-efficacy beliefs regarding the comprehension of American literature revealed different information. The following three questions all required only the first two levels of thinking/learning - knowledge and comprehension:

Question #1 – How well can you identify all the key points when reading text from your American literature book? The respondent would have to know what a key point is and then comprehend the text.

Question #2 – How well can you understand text, (in any form), in your American literature book when you put a lot of effort in? This question is primarily asking the respondent about their comprehension.

Question #5 – How well can you understand the meaning of each sentence when you read? This question is asking the respondent specifically about their sentence by sentence comprehension.

The two remaining questions that did not show an increase in the self-efficacy beliefs regarding the comprehension of American literature, still only required the first three levels of thinking/learning – knowledge, comprehension, and application:

Question #3 – While reading text from your American literature book, how well can you identify other important references that you may consider reading? This question requires the respondent to know what important references are, understand the text, and then use application to identify the important references.

Question #6 – How well can you recall the most important points when you have finished reading text from your American literature book? This question requires the respondent to know what important points are, comprehend the text, and then use application to recall the important points.

The results demonstrated that the two-part intervention of aesthetic reading and aesthetically-evoked reader response writing had positive effects on students' self-efficacy beliefs relevant to the higher-order thinking/learning domains or skills involved in the comprehension of American literature, as analyzed according to

Bloom's Taxonomy (1956). Thus, this study provides preliminary support for Rosenblatt's (1995) aesthetic reading and aesthetically-evoked reader response writing strategy. Rosenblatt's work has been enriched by testing and finding support for her work in the unique setting of South Florida where it had not been examined previously.

Research Hypothesis Three

Research hypothesis three was not supported by the results of this study. Although this hypothesis was guided by various studies (Pajares & Johnson, 1996; Pajares & Miller, 1994, 1995; Tomte & Hatlevik, 2011) that indicated differences between the self-efficacy beliefs of male and female participants when other factors were the same, the findings of this study were not supportive. As measured by the CRAL, there was not a significant (sex) x (treatment) interaction between the mean posttest level of self-efficacy beliefs regarding American literature for participants who have read selections aesthetically and written aesthetically-evoked reader responses and the mean posttest level of self-efficacy beliefs regarding American literature for participants who do not read selections aesthetically and write aesthetically-evoked reader responses.

Implications for Practice

Research Hypothesis One

The results of this study partially support research hypothesis one, which states that there is a positive relationship between aesthetically-evoked reader responses and students' self-efficacy beliefs relevant to American literature. Understanding that we must be extremely cautious about generalizing beyond the sample of this quasi-experimental study, aesthetic reading of literature that is coupled with aesthetically-evoked reader response assignments might be considered for implementation as a strategy to raise self-efficacy beliefs regarding literature. One implication for practice that might be utilized by all ELAR teachers was revealed upon an examination of the results of each reader response assignment that was given to the treatment group. Significant effects on the students' self-efficacy beliefs were particularly evident in one of the assignments. The researcher had chosen excerpts from Jack London's (1915) novel, *The Call of the Wild*, for the practice sessions with the treatment group. The researcher poses some possible explanations for these results.

The researcher's past classroom experiences with Jack London's novel, *The Call of the Wild* (London, 1915) had indicated that high school students usually enjoyed both the language and the action of this novel. The results may imply that teachers (districts and states) should be more selective about the literature that is selected for the required reading. The timing of those selections should probably be more delicately handled, particularly when the texts are difficult for the students because of such things as more formal language. There should probably be more of a balance in the curriculum, such that students work with the difficult texts for an interval of time, but then are allowed an authentic use of print experience with another, more enjoyable text. This text could be from the overall category, such as American literature, but from a different time period or from a different genre. *The Call of the Wild,* (1915) is classified as an American novel, but the time period of the novel was more recent than the literature texts of the previous week. The novel was also prose, not poetry, and students had already voiced their sentiments about poetry, asked if we were going to have to read poetry, and for the most part, were already adamantly against it. They strongly believed that it would be too hard to understand.

The teacher and researcher conferred daily during the study as well as after the study's conclusion. Before the results had been analyzed some professional conclusions had been discussed. As experienced English teachers, they surmised, based on the classroom comments, that the treatment students enjoyed the novel during the practice sessions so much, that the switch to the required Walt Whitman poetry was really disappointing to them. Possibly, the results of the study's hypothesis one would have been even more positive for this assignment if it had *followed* Whitman's poetry rather than preceded it. Would the results have changed significantly if poetry or a not-so-interesting novel had been used for the practice sessions, instead of the well-liked, *The Call of the Wild* (London, 1915)? It would be interesting to test this notion through a future research study.

Students had provided support for the above question. At the beginning of the first modeling and practice session, quite a few students had remarked that there were movie versions of the novel, *The Call of the Wild* (London, 1915), and they were excited about reading the excerpts. The researcher found out later in the study period that several students had checked-out *The Call of the Wild* (London, 1915) from the media center which was a very positive happening. After all, high school students are adolescents, not adults, and educators involved in creating and following the curriculum should never lose sight of that reality. The building of self-efficacy beliefs towards anything relevant to the comprehension of literature is an extremely important factor in helping all students succeed in school. Guthrie and Wigfield (2000) indicated that self-efficacy beliefs of students and engagement must be addressed for any literacy instruction to be effective. In addition, Alvermann (2001, 2003), Kamil et al. (2000), and Linnenbrink & Pintrich, 2003) held that the higher students' self-efficacy beliefs are, the more likely they are to do school-related reading assignments.

Research Hypothesis Two

The results of this study partially supported research hypothesis two: the mean posttest level of self-efficacy beliefs regarding American literature for participants who read selections aesthetically and wrote aesthetically-evoked reader responses were significantly higher than the mean posttest level of self-efficacy beliefs regarding American literature for participants who had not read selections aesthetically nor write aesthetically-evoked reader responses. An ANCOVA was run on each of the 12 self-efficacy questions on the CRAL. First, there was not a significant main sex effect; the (sex) x (treatment) group interaction was not significant as well on any of the twelve items. However, seven of the twelve ANCOVAs showed significant, positive effects of the intervention (treatment) of aesthetic reading and aesthetically-evoked reader responses. When analyzed using Bloom's Taxonomy (1956), six of the seven questions demonstrated that three or more higher-order thinking/learning skills were required.

The research hypothesis two results could have implications for both the curriculum and the instruction in ELAR classrooms. The national drive to implement The Common Core State Standards (CCSSI; NGACBP & CCSSO, 2010), is underway. The CCSSI fully explains that students must develop higher-order thinking/learning skills in order to be prepared for any type of postsecondary education or career training in their document, " Common Core State Standards Initiative: Preparing America's Students for College and Career" (2012). Being mindful of the generalizability of this preliminary research study, albeit quasi-experimental, the results of this study with primarily Hispanic students indicate that the strategy of aesthetic reading and writing aesthetically-evoked reader responses may have promise as a tool in helping students develop these higher-order thinking/learning skills.

ELAR teachers in all levels of instruction, elementary, middle, and high school should explore the possibility of adding the aesthetic reading/response writing strategy to the curriculum. The two-part strategy is probably adaptable to almost any literature and to many levels of students. Teachers could also explore the utilization of this authentic use of print activity for the purpose of encouraging and motivating their students to participate in independent reading. Engaging students in aesthetic reading and writing aesthetically-evoked reader responses on books and magazines that they choose could be positive in many ways. This strategy provides students with a medium for their unique voices through their own transactions with the text as written in reader responses. Perhaps students could receive positive feedback about their transactions with the text instead of taking a quiz? This type of feedback might be useful for building the mastery experiences that support student efficaciousness. This activity could also support another means of communication with teachers should the teachers decide to incorporate individualized conferences into their planning. Students could be increasing their self-efficacy beliefs about their reading comprehension, and they could also be developing skills in the higher-order thinking/learning domains of ELAR.

Furthermore, using the strategy of reading aesthetically and writing aesthetically-evoked reader responses to possibly increase students' levels of self-efficacy beliefs regarding higher-level thinking tasks might be applied to other subject areas. Allowing students to aesthetically read books, magazines and articles that relate to other subject areas, especially of their own choosing, and assigning aesthetically-evoked reader responses as they read could produce beneficial effects for the students by increasing their self-efficacy beliefs about higher-order thinking skills in those academic areas. Some researchers (Alvermann, 2001, 2003; Kamil et al., 2000; Linnenbrink & Pintrich, 2003) have indicated that students with higher self-efficacy beliefs regarding their comprehension of material are more likely to be engaged and attempt academic reading assignments. In addition, addressing the factors of students' self-efficacy beliefs and students' engagement are necessary for effective literacy instruction (Guthrie & Wigfield, 2000). These indicators all point towards higher academic achievement.

Finally, professional development about aesthetic reading and writing aesthetically-evoked reader responses should probably be offered to all teachers but especially to ELAR teachers. In the researcher's years as an ELAR educator, she has rarely heard, (if ever), other ELAR teachers saying that they had enough strategies to do their very difficult, complicated, and demanding job properly. It appears that the high-stakes testing and accountability movement will be around for a considerable amount of time. The provision of professional development about this study's intervention strategy would offer ELAR teachers a way to balance testing strategies with an authentic use of print strategy that gives students a chance to voice their unique perspectives about texts. This study's reader responses developed in uniqueness, complexity, and overall richness as the study progressed.

Research Hypothesis Three

This hypothesis was guided by various studies (Pajares & Johnson, 1996; Pajares & Miller, 1994, 1995; Tomte & Hatlevik, 2011) that indicated differences between the self-efficacy beliefs of male and female participants when other factors were the same. The findings of this study were not supportive because there was no significant (sex) x (treatment) interaction in this study. The implication for practice might be that this type of interaction may be significant with participants from other age groups, in other subject areas, in higher-level classes, in classes that are predominantly female, or in classes that are not predominantly Hispanic.

Implications for Research

This study's results suggest multiple implications for future research. Of paramount concern, research needs to continue on the nature of the self-efficacy construct, specifically as it relates to adolescents, resiliency, academic work achievement, and Hispanics. This study is the only one known by the researcher to examine self-efficacy beliefs relative to aesthetic reading and aesthetically-evoked reader responses in a particular subject area; therefore, it may be interesting to explore the replication of this study using populations that are not predominantly Hispanic. Those of other ages, such as those in elementary and middle school, might be considered for the participants in future studies. Participants in studies could also be from other socio-economic statuses, such as middle and high levels, and other academic class levels, such as honors, AP, exceptional student education (ESE) and college classes. The study could also be tested in other academic subject areas: math, science, social studies, art, and music by adding an independent reading requirement. The same study could be run, but with a much longer amount of time allotted; longitudinal studies would be particularly interesting due to the complexity of the self-efficacy construct.

It would be extremely interesting to explore the incorporation of Rosenblatt's strategy of aesthetic reading and aesthetically-evoked reader response (1938, 1978, 1993, 1995) into the currently-used, efferent-based instruction in high school ELAR classes. This would be especially informative and add to the field of knowledge if different academic levels of classes were used.

More research is clearly indicated. The field could benefit with further testing of the CRAL measure used in this research. Because of the relatively small overall sample, factor-analytic techniques could not be used to test the psychometric qualities of the measure beyond testing for Cronbach's alphas (Tabachnick & Fidell, 2007). Factor analysis would be used to speak to the construct validity of the measure. As a rule of thumb, Tabachnick and Fidell recommended at least 200 participants when factor analysis is required; the sample of 62 participants in this research falls far short of this goal. Future research should be designed therefore to sample 200 or more participants to support further instrument development (some methods scholars suggest that participant-to-variable ratios of 5-to-1 would be sufficient for factor-analytic work [e.g., Kline, 1994]; as the CRAL had 12 items, then 60 participants could be sufficient. Still, correlational work, like factor analysis, tends to be less reliable when the coefficients are estimated from small samples; hence, the recommendation for samples of 200 or more). Moreover, future studies should focus on the role of students' self-efficacy beliefs regarding higher-order thinking/learning tasks in most if not all subject areas. If supported by this research, further research should be undertaken concerning appropriate strategies for addressing the levels(s) of self-efficacy beliefs that are beneficial for student success and well-being. Finally, this research could be extended by linking the students' increased self-efficacy to their academic achievement.

Limitations of the Study

Several study limitations to this study must be considered. The participants of this study were enrolled in regular level English 3/American literature classes in a Title I magnet high school located in South Florida. Although the study population was mixed, the majority was Hispanic (56%), and the same percentage was also male. Care must be taken before generalizing the study's results to populations with other racial/ethnic or socio-economic populations or with populations that have a female majority. The study was also limited by the sample size ($N = 62$), so care should also be taken before generalizing to populations of other sizes. The allotted time for the study was also a possible limitation. This is because the length of the intervention may have been a factor in the treatment's ability to greatly increase the intervention group's self-efficacy beliefs regarding their comprehension of American literature and their success in English 3. This is based on the knowledge that the domain of American literature is vast and complicated, and the skills required to comprehend this literature with success are equally vast and complicated.

Summary

The results of this study provide empirical support for the hypothesis that engaging students in the specific intervention of aesthetic reading and writing aesthetically-evoked reader responses will increase the likelihood that students' self-efficacy beliefs towards the comprehension of American literature will improve. An increase in self-efficacy beliefs relevant to the comprehension of a novel, a text choice known to be of high interest and acceptance to adolescents was supported by this study. Specific increases in the self-efficacy beliefs regarding higher-order thinking/learning skills involved in comprehension were also supported. The results of the study also provided empirical support for the incorporation of an authentic use of print activity, reading aesthetically and writing aesthetically-evoked reader responses, into the English curriculum. These results also bring to the forefront the viability of curricula that is designed to simply mirror standardized tests. Every student deserves curricula that enhances and promotes his/her individual potential, but it must also provide a medium for students' voices to be heard. The results of this study indicate that the instructional strategy of aesthetic reading and aesthetically-evoked response writing has this potential.

REFERENCES

Allen, C. (1991). *Louise Rosenblatt and theories of reader response*. In J. Clifford (Ed.), The experience of reading: Louis Rosenblatt and reader response theory. Portsmouth, NH: Boynton /Cook.

Anyon, J. (1980). Social class and the hidden curriculum of work. *Journal of Education, 162*(2), 67-92.

Apple, M. W. (1996). *Cultural politics and education*. New York, NY: Teachers College Press.

Applebee, A. N. (1974). *Tradition and reform in the teaching of English*. Urbana, IL: National Council of Teachers of English.

Applebee, A. N. (1993). *Literature in the secondary school: Studies of curriculum and instruction in the United States*. Urbana, IL: National Council of Teachers of English.

Alvermann, D. E. (2001). Reading adolescents' reading identities: Looking back to see ahead. *Journal of Adolescent & Adult Literacy, 44*, 676-690.

Alvermann, D. E. (2003). *Seeing themselves as capable and engaged readers: Adolescent and Re/Mediated instruction* (Report No. ED-01-CO-0011). Naperville, IL: Learning Point Associates.

Bandura, A. (1977). *Social learning theory*. Englewood Cliffs, New Jersey: Prentice Hall.

Bandura, A. (1982). Self-efficacy mechanism in human agency. *American Psychologist, 37*, 122-147.

Bandura. A. (1986). *Social foundations of thought and action: A social cognitive theory*. Englewood Cliffs, NJ: Prentice-Hall.

Bandura, A. (1994). Self-efficacy. In Ramachaudran (Ed.), *Encyclopedia of human behavior* (pp. 71-81). New York, NY: Academic Press.

Bandura, A. (1997). Self-efficacy: The exercise of control. New York, NY: W.H. Freeman.

Bandura, A. (2006). Guide for constructing self-efficacy scales. In F. Pajares & T. Urdan (Eds.), *Self-efficacy beliefs of adolescents* (pp. 307-337). Greenwich, CN: Information Age Publishing.

Bandura, A. & Schunk, D. H. (1981). Cultivating competence, self-efficacy, and intrinsic interest through proximal self-motivation. *Journal of Personality and Social Psychology, 41,* 586-598.

Bernard, S. C., & Mondale, S. (2001). *School: The story of American public education*. Boston, MA: Beacon Press.

Bloom, B. S. (1956). *Taxonomy of educational objectives, handbook 1: The cognitive domain.* New York, NY: David McKay.

Brophy, J. E. (1990). Effective schooling for disadvantaged students. In M. Knapp (Ed.), *Better schooling for the children of poverty: Alternatives to conventional wisdom* (pp. 211-234). Berkley, CA: McCutchan.

Cadiero-Kaplan, K. (2002). Literacy ideologies: Critically engaging the language arts Curriculum. *Language Arts, 79,* 372-381.

Chall, J. (1967). *Learning to read: The great debate.* London, UK: McGraw Hill.

Christenbury, L. (1992). "The guy who wrote this poem seems to have the same feelings as you have": Reader response Methodology. In N. J. Karolides (Ed.), *Reader response in the classroom: Evoking and interpreting meaning in literature.* (pp. 33-44). White Plains, NY: Longman.

Chudowsky, N., & Chudowsky, V. (2007*). No Child Left Behind at Five: A Review of Changes to State Accountability Plans.* Retrieved from Chudowsky2_StateAccountabilityPlanChanges_010107.pdf

College Dictionary. (1988). Boston, MA: Houghton Mifflin.

Common Core State Standards Initiative: Preparing America's Students for College and Career, (2010). *The Common Core State Standards for English Language Arts & Literacy in History/Social Studies, Science, and Technical Subjects* Retrieved from http://www.corestandards.org/assets/CCSSI_ELA%20Standards.pdf

Common Core State Standards Initiative: Preparing America's Students for College and Career. (2012). Retrieved from http://www.corestandards.org/about-the-standards

Creswell, J. W. (2005). *Educational research: Planning, conducting, and evaluating quantitative and qualitative research.* Upper Saddle River, NJ: Pearson Education.

Cullinan, B. E. (2000). Independent reading and school achievement. Assessment of the Rose of School and Public Libraries in Support of Educational Reform. Retrieved from http://www.ala.org/mmgrps/divs/aasl/aaslpubsandjournals/slmrb/ /slmrcontents/volume32000/independent.cfm Retrieved from Center on Education Policy. (2007) website: http:/www.cep-dc.org/displayDocument.cfm?DocumentID-241

Delpit, L. D. (1988). The silenced dialogue: Power and pedagogy in educating other people's children. *Harvard Educational Review, 58,* 280-297.

Delpit, L. (2002). Introduction. In L. Delpit, & J. K. Dowdy (Eds.), *The skin that we speak* (pp.xix). New York, NY: The New Press.

Edelsky, C. (1991*). With literacy and justice for all: Rethinking the social in language and education.* London, England: Falmer Press.

Fine, M., Weis, L., & Addelson, J. (1998). On Shaky Grounds: Constructing White Working-Class Masculinities in the Late Twentieth Century. In D. Carlson, & M. W. Apple (Eds.), Power/*knowledge/pedagogy: The meaning of democratic education in unsettling times* (pp. 151). Boulder, CO: Westview Press.

Florida Department of Education. English III Course Description. (1997). Retrieved from http://www.fldoe.org

Florida Department of Education. Florida's Federal High School Graduation Rates 2010-2011. (2011a). Retrieved from http://www.fldoe.org/eias/eiaspubs/pubstudent.asp

Florida Department of Education. FCAT 2.0. (2012a). Retrieved from http://FCAT.fldoe.org/mediapacket/2012/default.asp

Florida Department of Education. Florida's Guide to Public High School Graduation. (2012b). Retrieved from http:www.fldoe.org/bii/studentpro/pdf/1112HS-Brochure.pdf

Florida Department of Education. Non-Promotions in Florida's Public Schools, 2010-2011. (2012c). Retrieved from http://www.fldoe.org/eias/eiaspubs/pubstudent.asp

Florida Department of Education. Free and Reduced Lunch (School). (2013a).   Retrieved from http://search.fldoe.org/default.asp?cx012683245092260330905%3Aalo41milgz4

Florida Department of Education. Membership By Race/Sex By School. (2013b). Retrieved from www.fldoe.org/eias/eiaspubs/xls/mem_schl_race_grd_gen1213.xls

Florida Department of Education. 2012-13 High School Grades. (2013c). Retrieved from http://schoolgrades.fldoe.org/

Florida Department of Education. 2013-2014 School Improvement Plan. (2014). Retrieved from http://sdhs.dadeschools.net

Florida Senate Bill. Chapter 2011-1, L.O.F. (2011). Retrieved from http: //www.flsenate.gov/Session/Bill/2011/0736

Fraenkel, J. R., & Wallen, N. E. (2009). How to design and evaluate research in education (7th ed.). New York, NY: McGraw Hill.

Frankenberg, R. (1993). *White women, race matters: The social construction of Whiteness.* Minneapolis, MN: University of Minnesota Press

Freire, P. (1970). *Pedagogy of the oppressed.* New York, NY: Herder and Herder.

Freire, P. (1998). *Teachers as cultural workers: Letters to those who dare to teach.* Boulder, CO: Westview Press.

Freire, P., & Macedo, D. (1987). *Literacy: Reading the word & the world.* South Hadley, MA: Bergin & Garvey Publishers, Inc.

Goodman, Y. M. (1982). Retellings of literature and the comprehension process. *Theory into practice*, 21, 300-307. Retrieved from http://search.proquest.com/docview/63493977?accountid=10901.

Guthrie, J. & Wigfield, A. (2000). Engagement and motivation in reading. In M. L. Kamil, P. B. Mosenthal, P. D. Pearson, & R. Barr (Eds.), *Handbook of Reading research* (Vol. 3, pp. 403-422). Mahwah, NJ: Erlbaum.

Hackett, G., & Betz, N. E. (1989). An exploration of the mathematics self-efficacy/mathematics performance correspondence. *Journal for Research in Mathematics Education, 20*, 261-273.

Hamill, S. K. (2003). Resilience and self-efficacy: The importance of self-efficacy beliefs and coping mechanisms in resilient adolescents. *The Journal of the Sciences, 35*, 115-146.

Hayes, S. (2013). *Moratorium on High Stakes Tests Is the Right Response to Common Core Implementation.* Retrieved from NCTE website: http://ncte.org/governance/hayes5-28-13

Houghton Mifflin (1998). *College dictionary.* Boston, MA: Author.

Howell, D. C. (1989). *Fundamental statistics for the behavioral sciences* (2nd ed.). Boston, MA: PWS-Kent Publishing.

Irvine, P. D. & Larson, J. (2007). Literacy packages in practice: Constructing academic disadvantage. In J. Larson (Ed.), Literacy as snake oil: New literacies and digital epistemologies (pp. 49-72). New York, NY: Peter Lang.

Irving, A. (1980). *Promoting voluntary reading for children and young people.* Paris, France: UNESCO.

Iser, W. (1974). *The implied reader: Patterns of communication in prose fiction from Bunyan to Beckett.* Baltimore, MD: Johns Hopkins University Press.

Kamil, M. L., Intrator, S. M., & Kim, H. S. (2000). The effects of other technologies on literacy and literacy learning. In M. L. Kamil, P. B. Mosenthal, P. D. Pearson, & R. Barr (Eds.), *Handbook of reading research* (Vol. 3, pp. 771-788). Mahwah: NJ: Erlbaum.

Karolides, N. J. (1992). The transactional theory of literature. In N. J. Karolides (Ed.), *Reader response in the classroom: Evoking and interpreting meaning in literature* (pp. 21-32). White Plains, NY: Longman.

Kline, P. (1994). *An easy guide to factor analysis.* New York: Routledge.

Kroger, L., Campbell, H. L., Thacker, A. A., Becker, D. E., & Wise, L. L. (2007). *Behind The Numbers: Interviews in 22 States about Achievement Data and the No Child Left Behind Act Policies.* Retrieved from http://cep-dcpublications/index.cfm?selectedYear=2007

Lane, J., & Lane, M. (2004). Self-efficacy, self-esteem, and their impact on academic performance. *Social Behavior and Personality, 32*, 247-256.

Langer, J. A. (1994). A response-based approach to reading literature. *Language Arts,71*, 203-211.

Langer, J. A. (1998). Thinking and doing literature: An eight-year study. *English Journal, 87*, 16-22.

Linnenbrink, E. A., & Pintrich, P. R. (2003). The role of self-efficacy beliefs in student engagement and learning in the classroom. *Reading and Writing Quarterly,19*,119-137. Retrieved from http://dx.doi.org/10.1080/10573560308223

London, J. (1915). *The call of the wild.* New York, NY: Grosset & Dunlap.

Luebke, S., & Lorie, J. (2013). Use of Bloom's taxonomy in developing reading comprehension specifications. ERIC. (No. EJ1013203 [Abstract]. Retrieved from http://files.eric.ed.gov

Luke, A. (2012). Critical literacy. *Theory into practice, 51*(1), 4-11. doi: 10.1080/00405841.2012.636324. Retrieved from http://dx.doi.org/10.1080/00405841.2012.636324.

Luthar, S., Cicchetti, D., & Becker, B. (2000).The construct of resilience: A critical evaluation and guidelines for future work. *Child Development, 71*(3), 543-562.

Malo-Juvera, V. (2012). *The effect of young adult literature on adolescents' rape myth acceptance.* (Doctoral dissertation). Retrieved from ProQuest. (UMI Number: 3517024).

Marshall, J. D. (1987). The effects of writing on students' understanding of literary texts. *Research in the Teaching of English, 21*, 30-63.

Mathews, J. (2000). Prepackaged school reform. *The School Administrator.* Retrieved from http://aasa.org/SchoolAdministratorArticle.aspx?id=14476.

MacDonnell, K. (1996). Making magic with reader response. In S. DeNight (Ed.), *The harvest.* Miami, FL: University of Miami.

McCabe, P. P., Kraemer, L. A., Parmar, R. S., & Ruscica, M. B. (2006). The effect of text format upon underachieving first year college students' self-efficacy for reading and subsequent reading comprehension. *Journal of College Reading and Learning, 37,* 19-42.

McCrudden, M. T., Perkins, P. G., & Putney, L. G. (2005). Self-efficacy and interest in the use of reading strategies. *Journal of Research on Childhood Education, 20*, 119-131.

McDougal Littell (2009). Florida. *McDougal Littell literature: American literature.* Evanston, IL: Author

Miami-Dade County Public Schools. Pacing Guides. (2012). Retrieved from
http://village.dadeschools.net/lvcontentitms_31/lvcontentitesm_31dispforr

Morrison, T. (1992). *Playing in the dark*. New York, NY: Vintage.

Moustafa, M,. & Land, R. E. (2002). The reading achievement of economically disadvantaged
children in urban schools using Open Court vs. comparably disadvantaged children using
non-scripted reading programs. 2002 Yearbook of the *Urban Learning Teaching, and
Research Special Interest Group of the America Educational Research Association,* 44-53.

Naseri, M. (2012). The relationship between reading self-efficacy beliefs, reading strategy use and
reading comprehension level of Iranian efl learners. *World Journal of Education, 2*(2), 64-
75.doi: 10.5430/wje.2.2.64 Retrieved from http://www.sciedu.ca/wje

National Commission of Excellence in Education. (1983). *A nation at risk: The imperative for
educational reform.* Retrieved from
http://datacenter.spps.org/uploads/SOTW_A_Nation_at_Risk_1983.pdf

National Council of Teachers of English. NCTE Position Statement. (2008). *The NCTE Definition
of 21st Century Literacies.* Retrieved from NCTE website:
http://www.ncte.org/posotopms/statements/21stcentdefinition

National Education Association. Committee of Ten. (1893). Retrieved from
http://tmh.floonet.net/books/commoften/mainrpt.html

National Governors Association Center for Best Practices & Council of Chief State School Officers.
The Common Core State Standards. (2010). Retrieved from
http://www.corestandards.org/the-standards

Nelson, J. M. & Manset-Williamson, G. (2006). The impact of explicit, self-regulatory reading
comprehension strategy instruction on the reading-specific self-efficacy, attributions, and
affect of students with reading disabilities. *Learning Disability Quarterly, 29,* 213-230.

Oxford Dictionaries Online. (2012). Retrieved from
http://oxforddictionaries.com/definition/english/efferent?q=efferent

Ozer, E. M., & Bandura, A. (1990). Mechanisms governing empowerment effects: A
self-efficacy analysis. *Journal of Health and Social Behavior, 22,* 200-415.

Pajares, F. (1996). Self-efficacy beliefs in achievement settings. *Review of Educational Research,
66,* 543-578.

Pajares, F. (1997). Current directions in self-efficacy research. In M. Maehr & P. R.
Pintrich (Eds.). *Advances in motivation and achievement* (pp. 1-49). Greenwich,
CT: JAI Press. Retrieved from
http://www.uky.edu/~eushe2/Pajares/effchapter.html.

Pajares, F., & Johnson, M. J. (1996). Self-efficacy beliefs in the writing of high school
students: A path analysis. *Psychology in the Schools*, 33, 163-175.

Pajares. F., & Miller, M. D. (1994). The role of self-efficacy and self-concept beliefs in mathematical problem-solving: A path analysis. *Journal of Educational Psychology, 86,* 193-203.

Pajares, F., & Miller, M. D. (1995). Mathematics self-efficacy and mathematical outcomes: The need for specificity of assessment. *Journal of Counseling Psychology, 42,* 190-198.

Pintrich, P. R., & Schunk, D. H. (1995). *Motivation in education: Theory, research, and applications.* Englewood Cliffs, NJ: Prentice Hall.

Pintrich, P. R., & Schunk, D. H. (2002*). Motivation in education: Theory, research, and applications* (2nd. ed.). Upper Saddle River, NJ: Merrill.

Powell, R. (2009). Introduction. In L. A. Spears-Bunton & R. Powell (Eds.), *Toward a literacy of promise: Joining the African-American struggle* (pp.1-19). New York: NY: Routledge.

Prat-Sala, M. e. & Redford, P. (2010). Self-Efficacy in Reading Scale [Database record]. Retrieved from PsycTESTS. Doi: 10.1037/t14516-000

Purves, A. C. (1990). *Testing literature: The current state of affairs.* ERIC digest. (No.   EDO-CS-90-08). ERIC Clearinghouse on Reading and Communication Skills. Retrieved from http://ericae.net/db/edo/ED321261.htm

Rosenblatt, L. M. (1938). *Literature as exploration.* New York: Noble and Noble.

Rosenblatt, L. M. (1978). *The reader, the text, the poem: The transactional theory of the literary work.* Carbondale, IL: Southern Illinois University Press

.
Rosenblatt, L. M. (1993). The transactional theory: Against dualisms. *College English, 55,* 377-386.

Rosenblatt, L. M. (1995). *Literature as exploration.* (5th ed.). New York, NY: The Modern Language Association of America.

Rosenblatt, L. M. (2003).). Literary theory. In J. Flood, D. Lapp, J. R. Squire, & J. M. Jensen (Eds.), *Handbook of research on teaching the English language arts.* (2nd ed. pp. 67-72). Mahwah, NJ: Lawrence Erlbaum Associates.

Rothstein, R. (2008). *A Nation at Risk Twenty-Five Years later.* Retrieved from http://www.cato-unbound.org/2008/04/07/richard-rothstein/a-nation-at-risk-twe

Sapir, E. (1921). *Language: An introduction to the study of speech.* New York, NY: Harcourt, Brace &World.

Sanders-Reio, J. (2010). *Investigation of the relations between domain-specific beliefs about writing, writing self-efficacy, writing apprehension, and writing performance in undergraduates.* (Doctoral dissertation). Retrieved from ProQuest. (UMI Number: 3409651).

Schunk, D. H. (1989). Self-efficacy and cognitive achievement: Implications for students with learning problems. *Journal of Learning Disabilities*, 22, 14-22.

Schunk, D. H. (2004). *Learning theories: An educational perspective*. New York, NY: Macmillan.

Schunk, D. H., & Pajares, F. (1995). The development of academic self-efficacy. In A.Wigfield & J. Eccles (Eds.), *Development of achievement motivation*. San Diego, CA: Academic Press.

Seeman, M. (1959). On the meaning of alienation. *American Sociological Review, 24,* 783-791. Retrieved from http://www.jstor.org/stable/2088565

Spears-Bunton, L. A. (1992). *Cultural consciousness and response to literary texts among African-American and European-American high school juniors* (Doctoral Dissertation). Retrieved from ProQuest. (UMI Number: 9312304).

Spears-Bunton, L. A., & Powell, R. (2009). *Toward a literacy of promise: Joining the African-American struggle*. New York, NY: Routledge.

Spring, J. (1997). *The American school*. New York, NY: The McGraw-Hill Companies, Inc.

Stowe, H. B. (1899). *Uncle Tom's cabin*. Boston, MA: Houghton Mifflin.
Tabachnick, B. G., & Fidell, L. S. (2007). *Using multivariate statistics* (5th ed.). New York: Pearson Publishing.

Tomte, C. & Hatlevik, O. E. (2011). Gender differences in self-efficacy ICT related to various ICT-user profiles in Finland and Norway: How do self-efficacy, gender and ICT-user profiles relate to findings from PISA 2006. *Computers & Education, 57*(1), 1416-1424.

U. S. Department of Education, (2002). *No Child Left Behind Act of 2001*. Retrieved from http://www2.ed.gov/policy/elsec/leg/esea02/index.html

U. S. Department of Education, White House, Office of the Press Secretary. (2009). *Fact sheet: The race to the top*. Retrieved from http://www.whitehouse.go/the-press-office/fact-dsheet-race-top

U. S. Department of Education, (2012). *Executive Summary*. Retrieved from http://www.ed.gov/sites/default/files/rttd-executivesummary.pdf

Van Keer, H. & Verhaeghe, J. P. (2005). Effects of explicit reading strategies instruction and peer tutoring on second and fifth graders' reading comprehension and self-efficacy perceptions. *The Journal of Experimental Education, 73*, 291-329.

Willinsky, J. (1990). *The new literacy*. London, UK: Routledge.

Zimmerman, B. J. (2000). Self-efficacy: An essential motive to learn. *Contemporary Educational Psychology, 25*, 82-91.

APPENDICES

APPENDIX A: PARENT CONSENT FORM

Appendix A

PARENTAL CONSENT TO PARTICIPATE IN A RESEARCH STUDY:

THE EFFECTS ON STUDENTS'SELF-EFFICACY BELIEFS REGARDING THEIR
COMPREHENSION OF AMERICAN LITERATURE WHEN AESTHETIC READING AND
READER RESPONSE STRATEGY ARE IMPLEMENTED

PURPOSE OF THE STUDY

You are being asked to give your permission for your child to be in a research study. The purpose
of this study is to examine the effects of a reading and reading response strategy on students' self-
efficacy beliefs, (how capable they feel they are), about comprehending American literature..

NUMBER OF STUDY PARTICIPANTS

If you agree to allow your child to participate in this study, he/she will be one of about 150 people
in this research study.

DURATION OF THE STUDY

Your child's participation will require about three weeks.

PROCEDURES

If your child participates in this study, we will ask your child to do the following things:

1.   Read the literature selections (that are required anyway), for their own connections and
impressions and opinions.

2.   Write reader responses that explain their own comprehension of the reading.

RISKS AND/OR DISCOMFORTS

The following risks may be associated with your child's participation in this study: There are no
risks in this study.

BENEFITS

The following benefits may be associated with your child's participation in this study: Your child will learn a different way to approach the reading that he or she is required to do for English 3 class. This could be a way of enjoying the reading that they have to do.

ALTERNATIVES

There are no known alternatives available to your child other than not taking part in this study. However, any significant new findings developed during the course of the research which may relate to your child's willingness to continue participation will be provided to you.

CONFIDENTIALITY

The records of this study will be kept private and will be protected to the fullest extent provided by law. In any sort of report we might publish, we will not include any information that will make it possible to identify your child as a subject. Research records will be stored securely and only the researcher will have access to the records. However, your child's records may be reviewed for audit purposes by authorized University or other agents who will be bound by the same provisions of confidentiality.

Your child will not be entering his/her name on any materials.

If we learn about serious harm to you or someone else, we will take steps to protect the person endangered even if it requires telling the authorities without your permission. If we have reason to believe that your child is being abused, we will report this to the Florida Abuse hotline. In these instances, we would only disclose information to the extent necessary to prevent harm.

COMPENSATION & COSTS

Your child will not receive a payment for this study. The assignments will be class assignments that will be part of their class grade and will take the place of some other assignments that your child would be required to do about the literature. Your child will not be responsible for any costs to participate in this study.

RIGHT TO DECLINE OR WITHDRAW

Your child's participation in this study is voluntary. Your child is free to participate in the study or withdraw his/her consent at any time during the study. Your child's withdrawal or lack of participation will not affect any benefits to which he/she is otherwise entitled. The investigator reserves the right to remove your child from the study without your consent at such time that they feel it is in the best interest.

RESEARCHER CONTACT INFORMATION

If you have any questions about the purpose, procedures, or any other issues relating to this research study you may contact Dr. Thomas G. Reio, Associate Dean of Graduate Studies, Florida International University, Tel: 305-348-2723, Fax:305-348-2081, Email: reiot@fiu.edu.

IRB CONTACT INFORMATION

If you would like to talk with someone about your child's rights of being a subject in this research study or about ethical issues with this research study, you may contact the FIU Office of Research Integrity by phone at 305-348-2494 or by email at ori@fiu.edu.

PARTICIPANT AGREEMENT

I have read the information in this consent form and agree to allow my child to participate in this study. I have had a chance to ask any questions I have about this study, and they have been answered for me. I understand that I am entitled to a copy of this form after it has been read and signed.

_____   _____

Signature of Parent/Guardian   Date:

_____

Printed Name of Parent/ Guardian

_____

Printed Name of Child Participant

_____   _____

Signature of Person Obtaining Consent   Date

PARTICIPANT REFUSAL

I have read the information in this consent form and do not want my child to participate in this study

Signature of Parent/Guardian   Date

_____   _____

Printed Name of Parent/Guardian   Date

APPENDIX B: CHILD ASSENT FORM

Appendix B

INSTRUCTIONS FOR COMPLETING THE CHILD ASSENT TO PARTICIPATE IN A
RESEARCH STUDY:

THE EFFECTS ON STUDENTS'SELF-EFFICACY BELIEFS REGARDING THEIR
COMPREHENSION OF AMERICAN LITERATURE WHEN AESTHETIC READING AND
READER RESPONSE STRATEGY ARE IMPLEMENTED

WHY ARE YOU DOING THIS STUDY?

We would like for you to be in a research study we are doing. A research study is a way to learn
information about something. We would like to find out more about ways to teach American
literature, and if these methods have effects on your feelings about comprehending the literature..

HOW MANY OTHERS WILL BE IN THIS STUDY?

If you agree to participate in this study, you will be one of 150 children in this research study.

HOW LONG WILL THE STUDY LAST?

Your participation will require three weeks of the regular English class time.

WHAT WILL HAPPEN IN THIS STUDY?

If you participate in this study, we will ask you to do the following things:

You will be reading the same literature as you normally would for the class, but you will be doing a
different type of assignment that will replace as assignment that you would normally do.

CAN ANYTHING BAD HAPPEN TO ME?

There are no risks.

CAN ANYTHING GOOD HAPPEN TO ME?

You may learn a way to approach the literature that you will like and benefit from as well.

DO I HAVE OTHER CHOICES?

There are no known alternatives available to you other than not taking part in this study.

WILL ANYONE KNOW I AM IN THE STUDY?

The records of this study will be kept private and will be protected by the researchers. There will be no identifying information on the short surveys that you will complete.

WILL I BE GIVEN ANYTHING FOR PARTICIPATING?

There is no payment. The literature is the same as what is required.

WHAT IF I DO NOT WANT TO DO THIS?

You do not have to be in this study if you don't want to and you can quit the study at any time. If you don't like a question, you don't have to answer it and, if you ask, your answers will not be used in the study. No one will get mad at you if you decide you don't want to participate.

WHO CAN I TALK TO ABOUT THE STUDY?

If you have any questions about the research study you may contact Dr. Thomas G. Reio, Associate Dean of Graduate Studies, Florida International University, Tel: 305-348-2723, Fax:305-348-2081, Email: reiot@fiu.edu. If you would like to talk with someone about your rights of being a participant in this research study, you may contact the FIU Office of Research Integrity by phone at 305-348-2494 or by email at ori@fiu.edu.

PARTICIPANT AGREEMENT

This research study has been explained to me and I agree to be in this study.

_____   _____

Signature of Child Participant   Date

_____

Printed Name of Child Participant

_____   _____

Signature of Person Obtaining Consent   Date

PARTICIPANT REFUSAL

This research study has been explained to me and I do not wish to be in the study.

_____   _____

Signature of Child Participant   Date

_____

Printed Name of Child Participant

APPENDIX C: DEMOGRAPHIC SURVEY

Appendix C

Demographic Survey

Directions – Complete in spaces provided.

1) Last five (5) numbers of your student I. D.

_____   _____   _____   _____   _____

2)   Age. _____

3)   Gender. (M) (F)   (Circle one.)

4)   Ethnicity (Check the one that applies to you.)

White (Non-Hispanic)   _____

Black (Non-Hispanic)   _____

Hispanic   _____

Asian/Pacific Islander   _____

Native American   _____

Multiracial   _____

5)   Have you retaken the FCAT (reading)?   Yes_____No_____
6)   If yes, how many times? _____ (Write the number)

7)   Do you have to take the FCAT Reading Retake this October?

Yes_____   No_____   I don't know_____

APPENDIX D: CONFIDENCE IN READING AMERICAN LITERATURE
SURVEY (CRAL)

Appendix D

Confidence in Reading American Literature Survey (CRAL)

Each statement in this questionnaire refers to your beliefs about your ability in various activities associated with reading American literature in your English 3 class. Do not spend too long thinking about each answer, just answer according to your initial thoughts and beliefs by checking the best (one) answer.

1.   How well can you identify all the key points when reading text from your American literature book?

_____not well at all

_____somewhat not well

_____somewhat well

_____very well

2.   How well can you understand text, (in any form), in your American literature book when you put a lot of effort in?

_____not well at all

_____somewhat not well

_____somewhat well

_____very well

3.   While reading text from your American literature book, how well can you identify other important references that you may consider reading?

_____not well at all

_____somewhat not well

_____somewhat well

_____very well

4.   After you have read a text, how well can you answer questions on it?

_____not well at all

_____somewhat not well

_____somewhat well

_____very well

5.   How well can you understand the meaning of each sentence when you read?

_____not well at all

_____somewhat not well

_____somewhat well

_____very well

6.   How well can you recall the most important points when you have finished reading text from your American literature book?

_____not well at all

_____somewhat not well

_____somewhat well

_____very well

7. Before you answer a question about the text, how well have you understood the meaning of the question?

_____not well at all

_____somewhat not well

_____somewhat well

_____very well

8. How well can you search effectively for relevant information in a text from your American literature book when you are asked to find support for an answer you have

given?

_____not well at all

_____somewhat not well

_____somewhat well

_____very well

9. When reading in your American literature book, how well can you write notes in your own words?

_____not well at all

_____somewhat not well

_____somewhat well

_____very well

10. If you cannot understand a text in your American literature book, how well can you understand it if you ask another student in your class about it?

_____not well at all

_____somewhat not well

_____somewhat well

_____very well

11. How well can you use a variety of different methods to enable your understanding of a text in your American literature book? (e.g., writing notes, printing pages from the online book and highlighting or underlining, etc.)

_____not well at all

_____somewhat not well

_____somewhat well

_____very well

12. How well can you select the most appropriate information from a text in your American literature book when you are asked to write an essay?

_____not well at all

_____somewhat not well

_____somewhat well

_____somewhat well

_____very well

APPENDIX E: SELF-EFFICACY BELIEFS IN READING (SER)

Appendix E

Self-Efficacy Beliefs in Reading (SER)

Each statement in this questionnaire refers to your beliefs about your ability in various activities associated with reading in Higher Education. Do not spend too long thinking about each answer, just answer according to your initial thoughts and beliefs.

1. How well can you identify all the key points when reading a journal article or academic book?

2. How well can you understand a journal article or academic book if you put a lot of effort in?

3. Whilst reading an article, how well can you identify other relevant references which you consider may be of further interest to read?

4. After you have read a text, how well can you answer questions on it?

5. How well can you understand the meaning of each sentence when you read?

6. How well can you recall the most important points (e.g., development of an argument) when you have finished reading a journal article or book chapter?

7. Before you critically evaluate a statement, how well have you understood its meaning?

8. How well can you search effectively for relevant background reading when writing an essay?

9. When reading, how well can you make notes in your own words?

10. If you cannot understand an academic text, how well can you understand it if you go to a lecture about it?

11. How well can you use a variety of different methods to enable your understanding of a book chapter or journal article? (e.g., highlighting, underlining, etc.).

12. How well can you select the most appropriate reading from a number of relevant articles and books?

Scoring:

- The original scale used a 7-point Likert-type scale.

- All items are positively loaded.

- The scoring for each participant is formed by calculating the mean across the 12 items.

Reference

Prat-Sala, M., & Redford, P. (2010). The interplay between motivation, self-efficacy and approaches to studying. *British Journal of Educational Psychology*, 80, 283-305. DOI:

10.1348/000709909X480563.

APPENDIX F: TWO COLUMN NOTES

Appendix F

Two Column Notes

Name:

Period/Date: Text title:

Quote (Please number)/Page#Response to selected quote (explain)

1._____   _____

_____   _____

_____   _____

_____   _____

_____   _____

_____   _____

_____   _____

_____   _____

_____   _____

_____   _____

_____   _____

_____   _____

_____   _____

_____   _____

_____   _____

_____   _____

_____   _____

APPENDIX G: READER RESPONSE RUBRIC

Appendix G

Reader Response Rubric

Teachers, please use this rubric for grading the reader responses. As you know from the pre-study workshops, the idea is to motivate the students by accepting their responses. Please remember that the study takes place over eight class sessions, and you will be responding and grading the responses as they are completed. Since the reader response grades will have effects on each student's overall average in your class, it is imperative that the grades are posted after the study is finished. Please note that plus and minus grades/points are at your discretion.

Responses are:	Grade:	Point Equivalent:

1) *complete (required number done)   A

    *show continued effort/thought

    * progressive improvement

    * not repetitive

    * written legibly

2) * almost complete   B

    * effort/thought on almost all

    * progressive improvement on most

    * rarely repetitive

    * written legibly

3) * missing a few   C

    * acceptable effort/thought

    * some progressive improvement

    * some repetitions

    * legibility okay

4) * missing quite a bit   D

    * effort/thought below acceptable

    * parts are copied

* legible but poor

5) * missing most   F

    * effort/thought poor

    * copied or semi-copied most

APPENDIX H: SUGGESTED FEEDBACK FOR READER RESPONSES

Appendix H

Suggested Feedback for Reader Responses

Teachers, this is a list of suggested comments that offer positive feedback for the reader responses that your students will be writing. As you already know from our pre-study workshops, the idea is to motivate the students by accepting their aesthetically-evoked responses to what they read. Of course, this does not mean that you will necessarily understand each student's connections to the texts, but it is important that you offer comments of support. Feel free to use your own!

Reader response is:	Suggested comments:
1. minimal	Nice try! More please!
2. obvious	Okay....and what else?
3. totally off track	Um...glad you wrote, but help me here! You must explain, Ok? Ask for help!
4. good effort	Way to go! Good try!
5. confusing	Good effort, but I'm confused...clue me in by explaining...I'm interested!
6. silly (immature)	Ok, you wrote...but, really? I'm disappointed in you.
7. students copied	Hey! I just read this exact response! Why?
8. really thoughtful	Wow! You're good at this! Keep it up! Yes! I like it!

9. sad or depressing

Thank you for sharing this. I appreciate your honesty.

10. no response/ several words

Hey! There are no right/wrong responses. Need help? I'm disappointed.

APPENDIX I: HELPFUL READER RESPONSE STARTERS

Appendix I

Helpful Reader Response Starters

Directions: Use any of the following starters when you have difficulty beginning your reader responses! You do not have to use them! You may also like to add a few of your own for future reference.

I think.....

I feel that.....

I noticed.....

I wish.....

I realize.....

A question I have is.....

I learned that.....

I wonder why.....

I discovered.....

This reminds me of.....

If I had written this.....

I liked the part....

I didn't like the part.....

This would be more exciting if.....

I would change this....

Use this space to add your own response starters for future reference. (Have fun!)

_____
_____
_____
_____
_____
_____
_____
_____
_____

_____

_____

_____

_____

Reference

MacDonell, K. Making magic with reader response. In S. DeNight (Ed.), *The harvest.*
    Miami, FL: University of Miami

Printed by
Schaltungsdienst Lange o.H.G., Berlin